EYE-WITNESSES TO NELSON'S BATTLES

EYE-WITNESSES TO HISTORY *EDITED BY JAMES HEWITT*

Eye-Witnesses to Nelson's Battles

Edited by James Hewitt

OSPREY PUBLISHING LTD

First published in 1972 by
Osprey Publishing Ltd., P.O. Box 25,
707 Oxford Road, Reading, Berkshire

© *Copyright 1972 James Hewitt*

SBN/85045/048/9

Photoset by BAS Printers Limited, Wallop, Hampshire
and printed in Great Britain by The Berkshire Printing Co. Ltd., Reading

Preface

Among the voices heard in this volume are those of Nelson himself (from his letters, journal, and *Sketch* of his life), his experienced colleagues, like Collingwood and Berry, boys on the men-of-war like Parsons and Lee, and old salts like John Nicol and Able Seaman Brown, and the military men, Colonels Drinkwater and Stewart. Stewart's is the only significant witness of the Battle of Copenhagen, and of the fascinating preparations for the assault, and thus worth giving at length. Nor could we forgo in little short of its full length, Surgeon William Beatty's noble account of Nelson's dying minutes. That this should stay, as written, without intrusion of the first person, seemed right; but it was thought desirable to convert John Theophilus Lee's more prosaic prose into the first person, thus eliminating his frequent references to himself as 'our young midshipman', 'our young hero', etc. Otherwise the accounts are as written, apart from a small amount of editing to improve narrative and flow, correction of obvious slips of the pen and the occasional jarring construction, and changing punctuation and spelling to conform with modern usage. Thus they can be read in the spirit in which they were written, rather than be regarded as historical curiosities.

Acknowledgements

The author and publishers wish to thank the following for permission to reproduce the illustrations appearing in this book:

The Trustees of the British Museum for figs. 3–5 and plates 2, 3, 5–14, 16–22 and 24–26; the Mansell Collection for plates 1 and 4; the Mansell Collection and the Gresham Committee for plate 15; the National Maritime Museum, Greenwich, for plate 23 (photographed by the editor in the Museum's grounds); the Council of the Society of Nautical Research and the editor of *Mariner's Mirror* for Rear-Admiral A. H. Taylor's plans of the Battle of Trafalgar (figs. 6, 7 and 8) which originally appeared in the *Mariner's Mirror* in 1950. The two plans of the Battle of St Vincent (figs. 1 and 2) are based on those appearing in Professor Christopher Lloyd's *St Vincent and Camperdown* and are reproduced by permission of the author and publishers, B. T. Batsford Ltd., London.

Contents

Illustrations

FIGURES   page

Early Service
1770–96

A sudden glow of patriotism was kindled
within me . . . 'Well, then,' I exclaimed,
'I will be a hero! and, confiding in Providence,
I will brave every danger!'
Nelson, at 17.

It was in 1797, in the battle fought with a Spanish fleet off Cape St Vincent, that the greatest figure in British naval history first gained fame, even greater glory following a year later with victory over the French at the Nile. By that time Horatio Nelson was a few weeks short of his fortieth birthday.

Apart from five frustrating years on half-pay in England immediately preceding the outbreak of war with Revolutionary France in 1793, Nelson had known trying and testing years of service at sea most years from the age of 12. He had commanded several small vessels. He had been in action several times, on one occasion losing the sight of an eye. He had had his first exhilarating taste of success, and known also the bitterness that follows setback and failure. Several times he put his life in danger. Twice he nearly succumbed to fever. He also survived moments of mental conflict in which he considered leaving naval service.

This crisis came after service on the Seahorse, *of 20 guns, in the East Indies, during which he saw his first action when that ship captured an armed ketch belonging to a Mysore potentate who had taken arms against the East India Company. He then went down with fever, and returned to England on the* Dolphin. *He was 17. The voyage gave time for self-questioning and reflection. A kind of epiphany occurred, and Nelson's destiny was set.*

I felt impressed with a feeling that I should never rise in my profession [he afterwards wrote]. My mind was staggered with a view of the difficulties I had to surmount, and the little interest I possessed. I could discover no means of reaching the object of my ambition. After a long and gloomy reverie, in which I almost wished myself overboard, a sudden glow of patriotism was kindled within me, and presented my King and Country as my patron. 'Well then,' I exclaimed, 'I will be a hero! and, confiding in Providence, I will brave every danger!'[6]

3

After the Dolphin *had been paid off in September 1776, Nelson served with convoys in the* Worcester *until the following April, when he stood examination for lieutenant.*

In pursuance, etc., of the 5th April 1777, we have examined Mr. Horatio Nelson, who by certificate appears to be more than twenty years,* and find he has gone to sea more than six years in the Ships and Qualities undermentioned:

		Y.	M.	W.	D.
Raisonable	Mid.	0	5	0	1
Triumph	Captain's				
	Servant	1	2	0	2
	Mid.	0	10	1	5
Carcass	Mid.	0	5	3	0
Triumph	Captain's				
	Servant	0	0	1	5
Seahorse	Mid.	0	5	2	6
	Able	1	7	1	6
	Mid.	0	4	3	2
Dolphin	Mid.	0	6	3	6
		6	3	1	6

He produceth Journals kept by himself in the *Carcass*, *Seahorse*, *Dolphin*, and *Worcester*, and Certificates from Captains Suckling, Lutwidge, Farmer, Pigott, and Robinson, of his diligence, etc.: he can splice, knot, reef a sail, etc., and is qualified to do the duty of an Able seaman and Midshipman. Dated the 9th April, 1777.

M.S., Captain John Campbell, Captain Abraham North.[19]

M.S. was in fact Nelson's uncle, Captain Maurice Suckling, who concealed the relationship from the other captains. Acting as an independent comptroller, he waited until the examining captains had made their decision before introducing his nephew, saying: 'I did not wish the younker to be favoured: I felt convinced that he would pass a good examination; and you see, gentlemen, I have not been disappointed.'

In the first known extant letter from Nelson, he wrote to a brother on 14 April 1777:

* He was, in fact, only 18.

I passed my Degree as Master of Arts (Lieutenant's Certificate) on the 9th instant, and received my Commission on the following day, for a fine frigate of 32 guns [the *Lowestoffe*]. So I am now left in the world to shift for myself, which I hope I shall do, so as to bring credit to myself and friends.[27]

In Jamaica, Nelson joined Sir Peter Parker's flagship, the Bristol, *rapidly rising from Third Lieutenant to First. France had now sided with America against Britain and the ship was employed, with but minor incident, off Cape François. Further promotion for Nelson came on 8 December 1778, when he was appointed Commander of the* Badger *brig, with action against American privateers. Six months later he was appointed Post-Captain into the* Hinchinbrook *and entrusted with command of the batteries at Port Royal.*

When Spain allied with France and America, a combined sea and land operation was mounted against the Spanish settlements in Nicaragua with the hope of taking the fort of St Juan, far up the river of that name.

I was chosen to direct the Sea part of it [wrote Nelson in *Sketch of My Life*, sent to the *Naval Chronicle* following the Battle of the Nile]. Major Polson, who commanded, will tell you of my exertions: how I quitted my ship, carried troops in boats an hundred miles up a river, which none but Spaniards since the time of the buccaneers had ever ascended. It will then be told how I boarded, if I may be allowed the expression, an out-post of the enemy, situated on an island in the river; that I made batteries, and afterwards fought them, and was a principal cause of our success.[29]

Actually the expedition had been far from a success. It was true that the fort was taken – but the season for attack had been ill-chosen, so that heat and sickness forced an early withdrawal. The enemy had scarcely suffered at all.

Nelson was again seriously ill, and travelled home to England on the Lion. *He convalesced at Bath nearly a year – an irksome time for an ambitious young man eager to be back at sea. But it must have been satisfying for him to muse on the near certainty that his appointment, a few months before his 21st birthday, as captain of a post ship (one carrying 20 guns or more) must ensure an eventual rise to flag rank.*

In August 1781, fit again, he was appointed to command the Albemarle *frigate of 28 guns, and spent a winter on convoy duty in the North Sea and Baltic. Then in the spring sailed with a convoy bound for Newfoundland and Quebec.*

Nelson:

From Quebec, during a cruise off Boston, I was chased by three French ships of the line, and the *Iris* frigate: as they all beat me in sailing very much, I had no chance left, but running them amongst the shoals of St George's Bank. This alarmed the line of battle ships, and they quitted the pursuit; but the frigate continued, and at sunset was little more than gunshot distant: when, the line of battle ships being out of sight, I ordered the main-top-sail to be laid to the mast; on this the frigate tacked, and stood to rejoin her consorts.

In October I sailed from Quebec with a convoy to New York, where I joined the Fleet under the command of Lord Hood; and in November I sailed with him to the West Indies, where I remained till the Peace.[29]

No mention in the Sketch *of a vain-glorious episode in the spring of 1783. As the war with America was coming to a close, Nelson, commanding a detachment of small ships, was seized by the idea of recapturing Turks Island, in the Bahamas, just lost to the French. The attack was clumsy and he was forced to withdraw, with casualties.*

At New York, when about to join Lord Hood's fleet, Nelson met Prince William Henry, third son of George III, later Duke of Clarence, Admiral of the Fleet, and King William IV. A lasting friendship developed between the two men. The Prince describes his first sight of the young captain:

I was then a midshipman on board the *Barfleur*, lying in the narrows off Staten Island, and had the watch on deck, when Captain Nelson, of the *Albemarle*, came in his barge alongside, who appeared to be the merest boy of a captain I ever beheld: and his dress was worthy of attention. He had on a full-laced uniform: his lank, unpowdered hair was tied in a stiff Hessian tail, of an extraordinary length; the old-fashioned flaps of his waistcoat added to the general quaintness of his figure, and produced an appearance which particularly attracted my notice; for I had never seen anything like it before, nor could I imagine who he was, nor what he came about. My doubts were, however, removed when Lord Hood introduced me to him. There was something irrestistibly pleasing in his address and conversation; and an enthusiasm, when speaking on professional subjects, that showed he was no common being.[6]

Nelson's only peacetime commission followed: commanding the frigate Boreas *in the West Indies. It led to his marriage to Fanny Nisbet, a young widow, niece of the President of Nevis Island. She had a small son whom Nelson adored. The marriage took place at Nevis on 12 March 1787; Prince William gave away the bride.*

Before the year was out the Boreas *was ordered home and Nelson's command ended. There followed five frustrating years on half-pay in England, mostly spent at Burnham, in Norfolk. But in January 1793, with war imminent, Nelson went to London and wrote to his wife on the 7th:*

Post nubila Phoebus – your son will explain the motto – after clouds come sunshine. The Admiralty so smile upon me that really I am as much surprised as when they frowned. Lord Chatham [First Lord of the Admiralty] yesterday made many apologies for not having given me a ship before this time, but that if I chose to take a 64-gun ship to begin with I should be appointed to one as soon as she was ready, and that I should as soon as in my power be removed into a seventy-four.

Everything looks war. One of our ships looking into Brest has been fired into. The shot is now at the Admiralty.[27]

He was right. War broke out with Revolutionary France on 11th February. The next twelve years brought almost constant active service for Nelson, and contained the victories for which he is renowned.

The 64-gun ship of the line to which Nelson was appointed was the Agamemnon, *which 'sails admirably; we think better than any ship in the Fleet'.*

The Fleet, under command of Lord Hood, had an early success, bringing false optimism that the war would not last long. The port of Toulon, with a French fleet intact in the harbour, was taken. Nelson was jubilant.

To his wife:

What an event this has been for Lord Hood. Such a one as history cannot produce its equal. That the strongest place in Europe and twenty-two sail of the line, etc. should be given up without firing a shot, it is not to be credited.

On Sunday August 25th a party deposed Admiral Trogoff and placed St Julien at the head of the fleet, manned sixteen sail of the line and were determined to come out and fight us who were only twelve sail, Lord Hood having sent away the other part of his fleet to give them the option. The fleet regret they did not.[27]

Hood sent Nelson to Naples to ask Ferdinand III for troops to secure Toulon.

From Naples Nelson wrote to his wife:

The King has twice sent for me, and I dine with him tomorrow after he has made me a visit which he is to do on board the *Agamemnon*. We are called by him the Saviours of Italy. I have acted for Lord Hood with a zeal which no one could exceed and am to carry from the King the handsomest letter, in his own handwriting, which could possibly be. This I got through Sir William Hamilton and the Prime Minister, who is an Englishman.[27]

There follows Nelson's first meeting with his future mistress:

Lady Hamilton has been wonderfully kind and good to Josiah. She is a young woman [then aged 26] of amiable manners, and who does honour to the station to which she is raised.[27]

Ferdinand III sent 6,000 troops to Toulon, but this did not prevent the French recapturing the port. Outstanding skill was shown by a young major of artillery, later to make a considerable name for himself in history – Napoleon Bonaparte.

Horatio describes the evacuation of Toulon to his brother William:

The particulars are as follows: that on the 13th a most numerous army covered the neighbouring hills, that Lord Hood had given notice to the inhabitants of the probable evacuation of the place, that on the 17th at eight o'clock at night a general attack was made on all our outposts which lasted all night; the foreign troops quitted them sooner than they ought to have, and the others were obliged to be abandoned the next morning, destroying the works, and spiking the guns, as well as a short time would allow.

Lord Hood attempted to rally the flying troops but it was impossible; our army retired into the town and Fort La Malgue. On the 18th the Neapolitan troops were ordered to embark, together with the royalists in as many troops as could be found. Then began a scene of horror which may be conceived, not described. The mob rose; death called forth all its myrmidons which destroyed the miserable inhabitants in the shape of swords, pistols, fire and water. Thousands are said to be lost.

In this dreadful scene and to complete misery, already at the highest, Lord Hood was obliged to order the French fleet, twenty sail of the line, twenty other men-of-war, together with the arsenal, powder magazines, etc. to be set on fire. One half of the town is said to be consumed with them.[27]

Lord Hood now looked to Corsica to provide a base for the British Fleet. Nelson reconnoitered the port of Bastia and recommended an assault. It was with a mixed force of marines and seamen that he landed to the north of the town on 4 April 1794. They laid siege to Bastia, which surrendered seven weeks later. Nelson felt his contribution to the success was overlooked, writing to his uncle, William Suckling:

Lord Hood and myself were never better friends – *nor although his letter does,* did he wish to put me where I never was – in the rear. The whole operations of the siege were carried on through Lord Hood's letters to me. I was the mover of it – I was the cause of its success.[27]

Another siege was quickly laid: this time to the fortified port of Calvi, on the north-west point of the island. The French garrison surrendered on 10th August, after holding out for six weeks.

Nelson described the siege in a letter to H.R.H. the Duke of Clarence:

The *Gazette* will tell your Royal Highness the general outlines of this siege which I believe is novel in its form. We landed about four miles to the westward of Calvi on June 19th; on July 19th we were in full possession of every outpost of the enemy with very trifling loss. Our batteries were erected with impunity in situations which the enemy ought to have prevented. Had they kept even a moderate look-out, our loss of men must have been great, every battery being within reach of grape-shot from its opponent.

On July 19th General Stuart [the military commander of the operation] sent in to ask if they had any terms to propose to him; their answer was the motto of the town – *Civitas Calvis semper fidelis.* We were then only 650 yards from the centre of the citadel, and they allowed us to erect very strong batteries under a mask without firing a single shot or shell.

On the 28th in the morning, our batteries, 560 yards from the citadel wall, were ready to open their force, consisting of twenty-one cannon, five mortars and four howitzers. General Stuart sent in to say he should not fire on the black flags [hospitals]. This note produced a negotiation, by which the enemy wanted to obtain a truce for twenty-five days; when, if no succours arrived, they agreed to surrender the town, frigates, etc. Lord Hood and General Stuart agreed to give them six days; but, while this was going on, four small vessels got in, which gave them hope, I suppose, of more effectual relief; for on the 30th day they rejected our offer; and our fire opened with all the effect we could expect.

On August 1st, at eleven o'clock, when much of the parapet was beaten down, and the houses in the citadel were either in ruins or in flames, the enemy hung out a white flag, and requested a suspension of hostilities for a few hours, to prepare terms. In twenty-four hours everything was settled – That on August 10th we were to be put in full possession, and the garrison and such of the inhabitants as chose were to be transported to Toulon, without being prisoners of war.

Thus is likely to end the attack of Corsica, the possession of which will, I hope, benefit our country.[27]

No mention that at Calvi he had lost the sight of his right eye, though not the eye itself. He did not write to his wife on the matter until five weeks after the injury occurred:

I left Calvi on the 15th. I hope never to be in it again. I was yesterday in Fiorenza and today shall be safe moored I expect in Leghorn, where I am to remain and recruit a worn out ship's company. Since the ship has been commissioned this is the first resting time we have had.

You may hear, therefore as it is all past I may tell you that on July 10th last a shot having struck our battery the splinters of stones from it struck me most severely in the face and breast. Although the blow was so severe as to occasion a great flow of blood from my head, yet I most fortunately escaped by only having my right eye nearly deprived of its sight. It was cut down, but is as far recovered as to be able to distinguish light from darkness, but as to all the purpose of use it is gone. However, the blemish is nothing, not to be perceived unless told. The pupil is nearly the size of the blue part. At Bastia I got a sharp cut in the back.[27]

Nelson was more concerned about not receiving full credit for his part in the siege of Calvi, as had happened after that at Bastia.

What degree of credit may be given to my services I cannot say. General Stuart and Lord Hood are as far asunder as the other generals. They hate us sailors; we are too active for them. We accomplish our business sooner than they like. We throw them and I hope ever shall both at sea and on shore in the background.[27]

The recognition he sought was not far away, but for a few more months the feeling of injustice was to rankle except when action fully commanded his attention. He was exhilarated by his first fleet action in March 1795. Seventeen French sail-of-the-line were sent out to engage the British in the hope that success would enable them to retake Corsica. The British had fifteen sail-of-the-line under the command of Admiral Hotham. The French showed reluctance to engage. Perhaps they were weighed down by the memory of their débâcle against Lord Howe the previous year at the 'Glorious First of June'. The speedy Agamemnon *led the chase.*

From the Agamemnon, *at sea, on 10th March, Nelson wrote to Fanny:*

We are just in sight of the French fleet, and a signal out for a general chase. We have but little wind and unfortunately the enemy are in-shore of us; however, I hope the Admiral will allow us to go on, and if the French do not skulk under their battery, I trust we shall give a good account of them.

Whatever may be my fate, I have no doubt in my own mind but that my conduct will be such as will not bring a blush on the face of my friends. The lives of all are in the hands of Him who knows best whether to preserve it or no, and to His will do I resign myself. My character and good name is in my own keeping. Life with disgrace is dreadful. A glorious death is to be envied, and, if anything happens to me, recollect death is a debt we must all pay, and whether now or in a few years hence can be of little consequence.

March 11th. Did not get sight of the French fleet this morning. I suppose they stood to the westward all night. The Admiral has just got information that the French fleet sailed from Toulon on March 1st and on the 8th off Cape Corse took the *Berwick* of 74 guns. They are certainly out looking for our convoy every moment expected from England.

March 12th. The French are now within four miles of *Agamemnon* and *Princess Royal*, our fleet ten miles from us, we standing towards our fleet, the enemy attempting to cut us off.[27]

The brush with the enemy came on the 14th. On the following day Nelson wrote to H.R.H. the Duke of Clarence:

Our fleet closed with *Ça Ira* and *Censeur*, who defended themselves in the most gallant manner; the former lost 400, the latter 350 men; the rest of the enemy's ships behaved very ill. Martini, the Admiral, and St. Michael, the Commissioner, were on board a frigate. The orders of the French were to defeat us and to retake Corsica; I believe they will in no respect obey their orders. Every ship fired red-hot shot; but we now know, from experience, they are useless on board a ship. The French bore away towards Toulon in the afternoon, and are now out of sight.[27]

Nelson to William Suckling:

The event of our brush with the French Fleet you will know long before this reaches you, and I know you will participate in the pleasure I must have felt in being the great cause of our success. Could I have been supported, I would have had *Ça Ira* on the 13th, which might probably have increased our success on the next day. The enemy, notwithstanding their red-hot shot and shells, must now be satisfied (or we are ready to give them further proofs) that England yet reigns Mistress on the Seas; and I verily believe our seamen have lost none of their courage; and sure I am, that had the breeze continued, so as to have allowed us to close with the enemy, we should have destroyed their whole fleet.[27]

And to his wife, a letter revealing much about Nelson's temperament and his conception of sea-warfare:

I am absolutely, my dearest Fanny, at this moment in the horrors, fearing from our idling here, that the active enemy may send out two or three sail-of-the-line, and some frigates, to intercept our convoy, which is momentarily expected. In short, I wish to be an Admiral, and in the command of the English Fleet; I should very soon do much, or be ruined. My disposition cannot bear tame and slow measures. Sure I am, had I commanded our fleet on the 14th, that either the whole French Fleet would have graced my triumph, or I should have been in a confounded scrape. I went on board Admiral Hotham as soon as our firing grew slack in the Van, and the *Ça Ira* and *Censeur* had struck, to propose to him leaving our two crippled ships, the two Prizes, and four frigates to themselves, and to pursue the enemy; but he, much cooler than myself, said, 'We must be contented, we have done very well.' Now, had we taken ten sail, and had allowed the eleventh to escape when it had been possible to have got at her, I could never have called it well done: we should have had such a day, as I believe the annals of England never produced.[27]

For his part in his first fleet action Nelson received the honorary appointment Colonel of Marines. He had another encounter with the French Fleet less than four months later, and felt further frustration.

To H.R.H. the Duke of Clarence:

The *Agamemnon* was sent from Fiorenzo with a small squadron of frigates to co-operate with the Austrian General de Vins in driving the French out of the Riviera of Genoa, at the beginning of

July. On the 6th, I fell in with the French Fleet of seventeen sail-of-the-line and six frigates; they chased me twenty-four hours, and close over to St Fiorenzo, but our Fleet could not get out to my assistance. However, on the 8th, in the morning, Admiral Hotham sailed with twenty-three sail-of-the-line; and on the 13th, at daylight, got sight of the enemy, about six leagues south of the Hieres Islands. A signal was then made for a general chase. At noon, the *Victory*, Admiral Man, with *Captain, Agamemnon, Cumberland, Defence*, and *Culloden*, got within gun-shot of the enemy; when the west wind failed us, and threw us into a line abreast. A light air soon afterwards coming from the eastward, we laid our heads to the northward, as did the enemy, and the action commenced.

It was impossible for us to close with them, and the smoke from their ships and our own made a perfect calm; whilst they, being to windward, drew in shore; our fleet was becalmed six or seven miles to the westward. The *Blenheim* and *Audacious* got up to us during the firing. The *Alcide* struck about half-past two, and many others were almost in as bad a state; but she soon afterwards took fire, and only two hundred men were saved out of her. At half-past three the *Agamemnon* and *Cumberland* were closing with an 80-gun ship with a flag, the *Berwick*, and *Heureux*, when Admiral Hotham thought it right to call us out of action, the wind being directly into the Gulf of Frejus, where they enemy anchored after dark.[6]

Nelson's squadron was now employed in blockading Genoa. On learning that a rumour was circulating accusing Britain's blockading captains of allowing cargoes to land in the Riviera of Genoa to supply the French Army, Nelson wrote indignantly to Lord Granville, Secretary of State for Foreign Affairs, on behalf of himself and his captains:

As this traitorous agreement could not be carried on but by concert of all the captains, if they were on the stations allotted them, and as they could only be drawn from these stations by orders from me, I do most fully acquit all my brother captains from such a combination, and have to request that I may be considered as the only responsible person for what is done under my command. Officers more alert, and more anxious for the good, the honour, of their King and Country, can scarcely ever fall to the lot of any commanding officer.

For myself, from my earliest youth I have been in the naval service; and in two wars have been in more than one hundred and forty skirmishes and battles, at sea and on shore; have lost an eye, and otherwise blood, in fighting the enemies of my King and Country; and, God knows, instead of riches, my little fortune has been diminished in the service: but I shall not trouble your Lordship further at present, than just to say – that at the close of this campaign, where I have had the pleasure to receive the approbation of the generals of the Allied Powers; when I expected and hoped, from the representation of His Majesty's ministers, that His Majesty would have graciously condescended to have favourably noticed my earnest desire to serve Him, and when, instead of all my fancied approbation, to receive an accusation of a most traitorous nature – it has almost been too much for me to bear. Conscious innocence, I hope, will support me.[6]

An event now occurred which marked a turning point in Nelson's fortunes. In Admiral Sir John Jervis, who replaced Admiral Hotham as Commander-in-Chief of the Mediterranean Fleet, Nelson found a leader after his own heart: a man of strong discipline and personality, totally dedicated to naval service. And a man well-equipped to recognize real merit in his captains. He hoisted his flag in the Victory *in June 1795.*

'Poor old Agamemnon' *being badly in need of a refit, a year later Nelson shifted his pendant to the* Captain, *of 74 guns, commanded by the New York born Ralph Miller.*

In October 1796, after observing their neighbour's land successes, Spain joined forces with Revolutionary France against Britain, at once making exceedingly difficult the position of the British in the Mediterranean. The French had line of battle ships at Toulon, the Spaniards at Cadiz and Cartagena. Shortage of supplies was the main problem weighing on the British government. They decided to evacuate their bases in Corsica and Elba, and to withdraw Jervis's fleet from the Mediterranean.

Jervis entrusted the task of taking off the garrison at Elba to Nelson. Mutual liking and respect had developed between the older and younger man. On 10th December at Gibraltar, Nelson transferred his commodore's pendant to Captain George Cockburn's La Minerve *– a French frigate of 38 guns, captured at Toulon. With her sailed the 32-gun frigate* Blanche. *Ten days later, off Cartagena, they met up with two larger Spanish frigates guarding the Spanish Fleet commanded by Admiral José de Cordova. There ensued a fierce engagement between* Minerve *and one of the enemy frigates, the 40-gun* Sabina, *whose captain, Don Jacobo Stuart, was a descendant of James II.*

Nelson wrote of the encounter to his brother, Reverend Mr Nelson.

When I hailed the Don, and told him: 'This is an English frigate', and demanded his surrender or I would fire into him, his answer was noble, and such as became the illustrious family from which he is descended.

'This is a Spanish frigate,' replied Stuart stoutly. 'And you may begin as soon as you please.'

I have no idea of a closer or a sharper battle. The force to a gun the same, and nearly the same number of men, we having 250. I asked him several times to surrender during the action, but his answer was – 'No, sir, not whilst I have the means of fighting left'. When only himself and his officers were left alive, he hailed and said he would fight no more, and begged that I would stop firing. The next frigate was *La Ceres*, of 40 guns, who did not choose to fight much. Not a mast, yard, sail or rope but is hacked to pieces.[6]

The fight had indeed been a fierce one. Stuart had 164 men killed or wounded. Lieutenants Culverhouse and Hardy boarded the prize, but had scarcely done so and Minerve *taken her in tow when Captain Cockburn discovered a Spanish ship-of-the-line and two others (attracted by the sounds of the two-hour battle) approaching fast. The crippled* Minerve *had to hastily abandon her prize, together with the boarding party, and sheer off.*

The two British frigates reached Elba safely and took off Sir Gilbert Elliot and his staff. On reaching Gibraltar Don Jacobo Stuart was exchanged for Lieutenants Culverhouse and Hardy and Minerve *set off on 11th February to an appointment with Jervis off Cape St Vincent.* Minerve *was chased by* Le Terrible *and another Spanish ship-of-the-line, and prepared for action. An incident in the Straits established a lasting bond of friendship between Nelson and Hardy, whose kiss he was to receive in his dying moment at the Battle of Trafalgar.*

Nelson sat down to dinner with officers and guests that included Colonel John Drinkwater, one of the military officers evacuated from Elba. The latter had just congratulated Hardy on no longer being a prisoner of war (on the now pursuing Terrible*) when there was a cry of 'Man overboard!'.*

The officers of the ship ran on deck [wrote Drinkwater]. I, with others, ran to the stern windows to see if anything could be observed of the unfortunate man. We had scarcely reached them before we noticed the lowering of the jolly-boat, in which was my late neighbour, Hardy, with a party of sailors; and before many seconds had elapsed, the currents of the Straits had carried the jolly-boat far astern of the frigate towards the Spanish ships. Of course, the first object was to recover, if possible, the fallen man, but he was never seen again. Hardy soon made a signal to that effect, and the man was given up as lost. The attention of every person was now turned to the safety of Hardy and his boat's crew. Their situation was extremely perilous, and their danger was every instant increasing from the fast sailing of the headmost ship in the chase, which by this time had approached nearly within gun-shot of the *Minerve*. The jolly-boat's crew pulled 'might and main' to regain the frigate, but made little progress against the current of the Straits.

At this crisis, Nelson, casting an anxious look at the hazardous situation of Hardy and his companions, exclaimed, 'By God! I'll not lose Hardy. Back the mizen topsail.' No sooner said than done, the *Minerve*'s progress was retarded, having the current to carry her down towards Hardy and his party, who seeing this spirited manoeuvre to save them from returning to their old quarters on board the *Terrible*, naturally redoubled their exertions to rejoin the frigate.

To the landsmen on board the *Minerve* an action now appeared to be inevitable; and so, it would appear, thought the enemy, who surprised and confounded by this daring manoeuvre of the Commodore (being ignorant of the accident that led to it), must have constructed it into a direct challenge. Not conceiving, however, a Spanish ship of the line to be an equal match for a British frigate, with Nelson on board of her, the captain of the *Terrible* suddenly shortened sail, in order to allow his consort to join him, and thus afforded time for the *Minerve* to drop down to the jolly-boat to take out Hardy and the crew; and the moment they were on board the frigate, orders were given again to make sail.

Being now under studding-sails, and the widening of the Straits allowing the wind to be brought more on the *Minerve*'s quarter, the frigate soon regained the lost distance, and in a short time we had the satisfaction to observe that the dastardly Don was left far in our wake; and at sunset, by steering further to the southward, we lost sight of him and his consort altogether.[10]

Minerve's troubles, however, were not yet over. That night she ran into fog, and on its lifting Nelson found they were surrounded by several large enemy ships. Skilled seamanship, making the most of the poor visibility, enabled the British frigates to escape and join Sir John Jervis's fleet off Cape St Vincent on 13th February. When Nelson informed his Commander-in-Chief on board the Victory *of the proximity of the enemy, he at once made the signal 'prepare for action'.*

The scene was set for the Battle of St Vincent, fought the following day, St Valentine's Day.

The Battle of St Vincent

14 February 1797

*Of all fleets I ever saw, I never saw one in
point of officers and men to our present one,
and with a commander-in-chief fit to lead
them to glory.*
Nelson to his wife.

British Ships at the Battle of St Vincent

(Key numbers refer to fig. 1)

Ship	Guns	Officers
Victory (1)	100 guns	Admiral Sir J. Jervis
		Captain R. Calder
Britannia (11)	100 guns	Vice-Admiral Thompson
		Captain T. Foley
Prince George (14)	98 guns	Rear-Admiral Sir W. Parker
Barfleur (15)	98 guns	Vice-Admiral W. Waldegrave
		Captain J. R. Dacres
Blenheim (5)	90 guns	Captain T. L. Frederick
Namur (10)	90 guns	Captain J. H. Whitshed
Captain (9)	74 guns	Commodore H. Nelson
		Captain R. W. Miller
Excellent (7)	74 guns	Captain C. Collingwood
Egmont (12)	74 guns	Captain J. Sutton
Goliath (13)	74 guns	Captain Sir C. H. Knowles
Irresistible (2)	74 guns	Captain G. Martin
Colossus (14)	74 guns	Captain G. Murray
Orion (3)	74 guns	Captain Sir J. Saumarez
Culloden (6)	74 guns	Captain T. Troubridge
Diadem (8)	64 guns	Captain G. H. Towry

FRIGATES

Ship	Guns	Officers
La Minerve	38 guns	Captain G. Cockburn
Lively	32 guns	Lord Garlies
Niger	32 guns	Captain E. J. Foote
Southampton	32 guns	J. McNamara
La Bonne Citoyenne	18 guns	C. Lindsay
Raven (brig.)	18 guns	W. Prowse
Fox (cutter)	12 guns	Lieutenant Gibson

Spanish Ships at the Battle of St Vincent

Santissima Trinidad	136 guns	Admiral J. de Cordova
Concepcion	112 guns	Admiral Morales de los Rios
Conde de Regla	112 guns	Admiral Conde de Amblimont
Mexicano	112 guns	Admiral P. de Cardenas
Principe de Asturias	112 guns	Admiral J. J. Moreno
San Josef (taken)	112 guns	Admiral F. J. Winthuysen (killed)
Salvador del Mundo (taken)	112 guns	D. A. Yepes
Neptuno	84 guns	J. L. Goicoechea
San Nicolas (taken)	84 guns	T. Geraldino (killed)
Atlante (taken)	74 guns	G. Vallego
Bahama	74 guns	Admiral D. de Nava
Conquistadore	74 guns	J. Butler
Firme	74 guns	B. Ayala
Glorioso	74 guns	J. Aguizze
Oriente	74 guns	J. Suarez
Pelayo	74 guns	C. Valdes
San Antonio	74 guns	S. Medina
San Domingo	74 guns	M. de Torres
San Firmin	74 guns	J. de Torres
San Francisco de Paulo	74 guns	J. de Guimbarda
San Genaro	74 guns	A. Villavicencio
San Ildefonso	74 guns	R. Maestre
San Juan Nepomuceno	74 guns	A. Boneo
San Pablo	74 guns	B. de Cisneros
San Ysidro (taken)	74 guns	D. T. Argumosa
Soberano	74 guns	J. V. Yanez
Terrible	74 guns	F. Uriarte

FRIGATES

Atocha	34 guns	*Matilda*	34 guns	*San Balbino* (urca)	20 guns
Brigida	34 guns	*Mercedes*	34 guns	*San Paulo* (urca)	20 guns
Ceres	34 guns	*Perla*	34 guns	*San Justa* (urca)	18 guns
Diana	34 guns	*Asuncion* (urca)	28 guns	*Vigilante* (brig.)	12 guns

Jervis's fleet, together and disciplined, awaited the enemy.

This early part of 1797 was a low point for British fortunes. The Mediterranean was now closed to British shipping; the garrisons on Corsica and Elba had been evacuated; Spain and the Italian states had allied with France. Britain's allies had suffered reverses on the Rhine and on the Po. A 27-year-old general was making a name for himself – Napoleon Bonaparte. There was a shortage of food in Britain due to the second successive harvest failure: in parts, actual starvation. With the French and Spanish fleets combining there was the distinct possibility of direct invasion of England – only atrocious weather had prevented an invasion of Ireland at Bantry Bay in January. Jervis and his captains knew that what was needed to raise the spirits of government and people was a resounding battle success.

Jervis was confident of victory, in spite of a series of recent disappointments and mishaps among his ships.

In November 1796, when the fleet had been off Corsica, he had sent Vice-Admiral Robert Man with some ships to collect provisions from Gibraltar. Man and the squadron defied orders and sailed for England. Jervis did not openly complain, but he must have felt Man's defection bitterly. An order awaited him on the fleet's arrival at Gibraltar on 1st December to evacuate the Mediterranean and base his fleet on Lisbon. Next a dreadful gale wrecked and sank the Courageux, with a loss of three-quarters of her crew. Then Zealous went aground and, after refloating, limped into dock for repairs, and Gibraltar ran on a reef and was sent to England for repairs. This was not the end of the fleet's misfortunes. When they reached the Tagus on 22nd December, due to a combination of bad weather and the absence of pilots, the 74-gun Bombay Castle ran aground and was totally wrecked, though the crew were saved – and the three-decker St George, of 98 guns, ripped her bottom on a shoal and was sent into dock for repairs.

Thus, in a matter of weeks, Jervis's fleet was reduced from fifteen ships to nine.

They sailed from Lisbon on 18th January, escorting a Portuguese convoy bound for Brazil for some days before leaving it to rendezvous off Cape St Vincent at the Mediterranean's exit, where they awaited the return of Nelson from his special mission and reinforcements from home.

Cape St Vincent is Europe's most south-westerly point, near to the port of Lagos. Ships pass from the Mediterranean through the Strait of Gibraltar, cross the Gulf of Cadiz, and round Cape St Vincent to sail north for the British Isles and western Europe. In the area six sea battles had already been fought earlier in the century, including Rodney's famous moonlight victory in 1780. And Trafalgar was to be fought 100 miles south-east of the Cape.

The expected reinforcements, under command of Rear-Admiral Sir William Parker, arrived on 6th February: the Prince George, Namur, Orion, Irresistible, Colossus, *and the frigate* Thalia; *also some frigates under Lord Garlies. These fresh and fast arrivals were to be placed in the van on St Valentine's Day.*

The fleet that Nelson had so remarkably passed through was that commanded by Admiral José de Cordova, which had sailed from Cartagena on 1st February, escorting four large merchant ships (urcas) carrying large quantities of mercury to Cadiz. Jervis first had word of the enemy's approach on 8th February. Confirmation came two days later, when Jervis told the Admiralty: 'I flatter myself we shall be able to deal with them.' Even with Parker's reinforcements, he was outnumbered nearly two to one – but in effectiveness as a fighting force the Spaniards just could not compare with the British Fleet's experience, discipline, and advance preparation.

Sir John Jervis, now aged 62, had run away to sea as a boy, and been brought back. His father (a treasurer of Greenwich Hospital) gave him twenty pounds and a suit of clothes and told him to join the Navy and make a name for himself if he could. The morning ceremony of the Colours is but one of the customs he introduced to the Navy. He disliked promotion through influence, and was quick to reward real merit where he saw it. He has a lasting claim to fame as the man who recognized Nelson's naval genius and gave him the chance to exercise it. Following the Battle of the Nile Nelson wrote to him on his own behalf and that of other officers: 'We look to you, as we have always found you, as to our father, under whose fostering care we have been led to fame.'

From the time of hoisting his flag in the Victory *in June 1795, to the day of the Battle of St Vincent, Jervis had improved the morale of the fleet, tightened discipline, and trained a fighting machine superior to the numerically stronger enemy. By insisting on greater cleanliness he reduced the amount of sickness among the crews. He kept his men on ship as much as possible, and on the alert. To the First Lord he was able to report: 'We have no relaxation in port, where we never go without positive necessity; the officers are all kept to their duty; no sleeping on shore, or rambling about the country; and when at sea we do not make snug for the night, as in the Western Squadron* (the Channel Fleet), *but are working incessantly by the lead to keep our position, insomuch as both mind and body are continually upon the stretch.' To sustain such efficiency, Jervis required officers of a similar attitude towards naval service as himself. 'Fortunately for me,' he told the First Lord, 'Commodore Nelson and several of the captains of the line-of-battle ships and frigates under my command are of a temper that will work to anything.' Several of these captains had figured in fighting service during the War of American Independence; some had fought under Howe at the 'Glorious First of June' 1794. Several were to be among Nelson's 'band of brothers' at the Nile.*

Back with Jervis's fleet again, Nelson transferred his pendant from Minerve *to the* Captain, *of 74 guns. The Commander-in-Chief gave the order 'Prepare for battle'; then held a dinner party on the* Victory *for Sir Gilbert Elliot, who, with Colonel Drinkwater, pleaded to stay to see the action. They witnessed the battle from their frigate.*

Information came through at intervals to Jervis in the early hours of the morning of the 14th that the Spaniards were close, the first news at 2.30 a.m. from a Scotsman commanding a Portuguese frigate. The sun rose to combat a thick mist, which soon lifted as the day advanced. At 6.30 a.m. the Victory's *log recorded: 'Discovered a number of strange sail to windward, supposed to be the Spanish fleet.'*

During the night Jervis had written his will. He was pleased at dawn to find his fleet together in close order, on which he congratulated his captains. He also told them: 'A victory is very essential to England at this moment.'

The three-decker Barfleur, *of 98 guns, flew the flag of Vice-Admiral William Waldegrave. Her captain was J. B. Dacres. Combining the duties of captain's servant and midshipman was G. S. Parsons, then aged 12 years. A boy's impressions are fresh and vivid, and Parsons was to write a lively account of the battle of St Vincent in his reminiscences:*

The 13th of February 1797 was employed by the British squadron, under Sir John Jervis, in getting ready for the ensuing fight. Grinding cutlasses, sharpening pikes, flinting pistols, among the boarders; filling powder, and fitting well-oiled gunlocks on our immense artillery by the gunners, slinging our lower yards with chains; and, in short, preparing a well-organized first-rate for this most important battle.

The men and officers seemed to me to look taller, and the anticipation of victory was legibly written on each brow.[32]

In mid-paragraph Parsons now favours us with a digression so delightful we should not forgo it:

It was my good fortune at that period to be in great favour with the vice-admiral; so much so that each day he personally took me to where the grapes clustered his cabin, and the oranges in nettings hung thick above my head, with strong injunctions only to eat what had begun to decay. I was then not quite thirteen, and strictly obeyed orders, *while he was in sight to enforce them*, otherwise a tempting peach, with its soft maiden blush, or the coarser red of juicy nectarine, diverted me from the straight and narrow path – I am sorry to reflect how frequently.

The admiral was a polished, good-natured gentleman, and always took me as midshipman of his boat when mustering the crews of the ships of squadron in rotation. We one morning went on board the *Excellent*, Captain Cuthbert, Collingwood, not then so celebrated as he afterwards became, and I, being tired of seeing John Marlingspike and Tom Rattling smooth down his front hair, and hitch up his trousers, preparatory to scraping his foot, with his best sea jerk, as he passed in review before the big-wigs, and pressed to go down by a brother mid., who felt proud of feasting the vice-admiral's aide-de-camp – and having internal conviction, as well as external, that the hour of noon had passed – the usual hour of dinner for young gentlemen – I, forgetting my proud station, stole from the vice-admiral's side, and was well employed in stowing my hold in the most expeditious manner with beef and pudding in the middy's berth, when all at once I heard, 'Pass the word for the vice-admiral's midshipman; his admiral and captain are towing alongside, waiting for him.'

This alarming information nearly caused me to choke, by endeavouring to swallow a large piece of pudding I had in my mouth, and with my cocked hat placed on my head the wrong way, I crossed the hawse of Captain Collingwood, who, calling me a young scamp, and some other hard names, which I have long since forgiven, assured me, in not a very friendly tone, that if I was his midshipman, he would treat me with a dozen by marrying me to the gunner's daughter. This did not restore my self-possession; for, being rather of an imaginative turn, I had a slight suspicion that Captain Dacres would very probably execute what his brother captain had hinted.

But oh, the storm when I opened the gangway! a typhoon or hurricane must have appeared a calm compared to it; and in my hurry to jump into the boat, the *Excellent* having steerage way, I alighted on my captain's old-fashioned cocked hat. He seemed paralysed with rage; and the vice-admiral, who had not before spoken, with a quiet smile told me to sit down, and asked me, in a kind voice, 'if my hunger was too great for his dinner?' I hung my head, like most culprits, and listened in silence to the captain's promised retribution; but I had a strong friend in the admiral, and was let off with a lecture as long as the main top-bowline.[32]

Parsons returns without pause to the battle story:

During the long night of the 13th of February, we heard many heavy guns to windward, and felt perfectly certain that they proceeded from the Spanish fleet, which could not be very remote. The day dawned in the east, and 'Up all hammocks, ahoy!'

resounded through the decks of His Majesty's ship *Barfleur*. Some were sent aloft to barricade the tops, while the remainder were stowed with unusual care as a bulwark round the upper decks. Great haze had prevailed during the night, and it still continued.[32]

As the morning mist began lifting, various British ships reported sight of the enemy. Jervis was on the quarter-deck of the Victory, *whose captain (and Captain of the Fleet), Sir Robert Calder, called the numbers of the enemy to the Admiral:*

'There are eight sail of the line, Sir John.'

'Very well, Sir.'

'There are twenty sail of the line, Sir John.'

'Very well, Sir.'

'There are twenty-five sail of the line, Sir John.'

'Very well, Sir.'

'There are twenty-seven sail, Sir John.'

'Enough, Sir, no more of that: the die is cast, and if there are fifty sail I will go through them.'[35]

Parsons:

Intimations of approaching battle were received by the British squadron with reiterated cheers; and so beautifully close was our order of sailing, that the flying jib-boom of the ship astern projected over the taffrail of her leader.

John Nicol, a veteran mariner, below deck on the Goliath:

Soon as we came in sight, a bustle commenced, not to be conceived or described. To do it justice, while every man was as busy as he could be, the greatest order prevailed. A serious cast was to be perceived on every face; but not a shade of doubt or fear. We rejoiced in a general action; not that we loved fighting; but we all wished to be free to return to our homes, and follow our own pursuits. We know there was no other way of obtaining this than by defeating the enemy. 'The hotter war the sooner peace', was a saying with us.

When everything was cleared, the ports open, the matches lighted, and guns run out, then we gave them three such cheers as are only to be heard in a British man-of-war. This intimidates the enemy more than a broadside, as they have often declared to me.

It shows them all is right; and the men in the true spirit baying to be at them.[30]

Colonel Drinkwater observed the battle from the frigate Lively:

The ships first discovered by the *Culloden* were separated from their main body, which being to windward, were bearing down in some confusion, with a view of joining their separated ships. It appeared to have been the British Admiral's intention, upon discovering the separated ships of the enemy's fleet, to have cut them off, if possible, before their main body could arrive to their assistance; and, with this in view, the fast sailing ships of his squadron were ordered to chase.

Assured now of the near position of their main body, he probably judged it most advisable to form his fleet into the line of battle, and the signal was made for their forming the line of battle a-head and a-stern as most convenient. A signal was made directing the squadron to steer S.S.W.

About twenty minutes past eleven o'clock the Admiral pointed out that the *Victory* (his flag-ship) would take her station next to the *Colossus*. Some variation in steering was afterwards directed, in order to let the rear ships close up. At twenty-six minutes past eleven o'clock, the Admiral communicated his intention to pass through the enemy's line, hoisting his large flag and ensign, and soon after the signal was made to engage.

The British van by this time had approached the enemy; and the distinction of leading the British line into action fell to the lot of the *Culloden*, commanded by Captain Troubridge. About half-past eleven o'clock the firing commenced from the *Culloden* against the enemy's headmost ships to windward.[10]

The attacking British were together in line; the Spanish ships were in poor order, with the convoy and its escort a considerable distance leeward of the main body. Moreover, three of Cordova's best ships – the Principe de Asturias, *112 guns under Admiral J. J. Moreno, the* Conde de Regla, *112 guns, Admiral C. de Amblimont, and the* Oriente, *74 guns – were so far out of order as to put them virtually out of the action.*

Parsons:

Captain Troubridge led the British line; and one more competent could not have been selected. Here we must admire that wonderful tact, and knowledge of human nature, possessed by Sir John Jervis. Naval etiquette has established the senior captain as better fitted to lead, from his experience, and he is so placed in the established order of battle; but practice has sometimes proved the fallacy of such a theory; and Sir John, without offending, placed at the head of his line, one of the most perfect seamen, though, as his subsequent end proved, too daring, even to rashness. This ill-fated officer took the *Culloden* home from Malta, when she had been declared not seaworthy, and tried the same in the *Blenheim* from India (in 1807), and has never since been heard of. But on February 14 no man could have led the British line better . . . .[32]

Nelson and Thomas Troubridge had been midshipmen together in the West Indies. Jervis held his 'honour and courage' to be 'as bright as a sword'. Culloden had been damaged shortly before the battle, but an exceptionally rapid repair enabled Troubridge's ship to join the fleet and lead the line through the gap between the Spanish main body and convoy and escort to leeward.

Parsons continues:

'I have a glimpse through the fog of their leeward line,' called Signal-Lieutenant Edghill, from the mainyard, 'and they loom like Beachy Head in a fog. By my soul, they are thumpers, for I distinctly make our *four* tier of ports in one of them, bearing an admiral's flag.'

'Don Cordova, in the *Santissima Trinidad*,' said the vice-admiral, 'and I trust in Providence that we shall reduce this mountain into a mole hill before sunset.

The British had formed one of the most beautiful and close lines ever beheld. The fog drew up like a curtain, and disclosed the grandest sight I ever witnessed. The Spanish fleet, close on our weather bow, were making the most awkward attempts to form their line of battle, and they looked a complete forest huddled together; their commander-in-chief, covered with signals, and running free on his leeward line, using his utmost endeavours to get them into order; but they seemed confusion worse confounded.

I was certainly very young, but felt so elated as to walk on my toes, by way of appearing taller, as I bore oranges to the admiral and captain, selecting some for myself, which I stored in a snug corner in the stern-galley, as a *corps de reserve*. The breeze was just sufficient to cause all the sails to sleep, and we were close hauled on the starboard tack, with royals set, heading up for the Spanish fleet. Our supporting ship, in the well-formed line, happened to be the *Captain*, and Captain Dacres hailed to say that he was desired by the vice-admiral to express his pleasure at being supported by Sir Horatio Nelson.

It wanted some time of noon when the *Culloden* opened her fire on the Spanish van, and our gallant fifteen, so close together, soon imitated her example. The roar was like heavy thunder, and the ship reeled and shook as if she was inclined to fall in pieces. I felt a choking sensation from the smell and smoke of gunpowder, and did serious execution on the oranges.[32]

Drinkwater:

As the British squadron advanced, the action became more general, and it was soon apparent that the British admiral had accomplished his design of passing through the enemy's line.

The animated and regular fire of the British squadron was but feebly returned by the enemy's ships to windward, which, being frustrated in their attempts to join the separated ships, had been obliged to haul their wind on the larboard tack: those to leeward, and which were most effectually cut off from their main body, attempted also to form on their larboard tack, apparently with a determination of either passing through, or to leeward of our line, and joining their friends; but the warm reception they met with from the centre ships of our squadron soon obliged them to put about; and excepting one, the whole sought safety in flight, and did not again appear in the action until the close of the day.

The single ship thus excepted wore and stood on the other tack, with the design of passing round the rear of the British ships, and of joining her friends in the main body to windward, which intention she accomplished. Her course lay between the British line of battle ships and the British frigates. In passing to windward of the latter, she presented so tempting an object to the *Lively*, that the gunner was so importunate to have one shot from a favourite gun, an eighteen-pounder in the midships, which he assured his lordship he was certain would hit the Don, that Lord Garlies consented to his request, and the old fellow, as well as all on board, was much gratified to see the shot strike the two-decker, near the fourth or fifth port-hole abaft. (We were afterwards informed that this shot killed and wounded four or five men, for in the after action, this ship, the *San Ysidro*, became a prize, and the *Lively* was ordered to take possession of her.) Finding herself thus within our range, the *San Ysidro* gave the *Lively* and the other frigates her broadside; but so badly were the guns pointed, that not one shot struck our ships, though many went through their sails.

Sir John Jervis, having effected his first purpose, now directed his whole attention to the enemy's main body to windward, consisting at this time of eighteen sail of the line. At eight minutes past twelve the signal therefore was made for the British fleet to tack in succession, and soon after he made the signal for again passing the enemy's line.[10]

Parsons:

The uproar and blinding appeared to me to have lasted a considerable time; but I judged more from my feelings than my watch, when I heard our active signal-lieutenant report the *Culloden*'s signal to tack and break through the enemy's line, and the fleet to follow in succession. Down went the *Culloden*'s helm, and she dashed through between the nineteenth and twentieth ship of the enemy.[32]

Troubridge had anticipated the order to tack, and had his answering flags broken immediately, to Jervis's delight. 'Look at Troubridge there!' Jervis shouted. 'He tacks his ship in battle as if the eyes of England were upon him; and would to God they were, for they would see him to be, what I know him to be, and, by Heaven, as the Dons will soon feel him to be!'

The other van ships followed Culloden, *tacking in succession, to again split and engage the enemy, with one exception.* Colossus *had*

The Battle of St Vincent 33

*her fore topmast shot away and, unable to steer a course, drifted
across the ship astern of her,* Irresistible, *forcing both her and the*
Victory *to swerve to avoid a collision.* Colossus *fell out of line and
became an encumbrance in the battle.*

Drinkwater:

The Spanish Admiral's plan seemed to be to join his ships to
leeward, by wearing round the rear of our line; and the ships
which had passed and exchanged shots with our squadron, had
actually borne up with this view.[10]

*In moving forward the rear ships of the British line had presented
Cordova with the possibility of uniting his split forces. It was at this
point that Nelson, in the* Captain, *third from the rear of the line,
gambled on one of the most startling tactical moves in the history of
battles at sea ever made in the face of normal naval procedure.*

Vice-Admiral Waldegrave in the Barfleur *astern of the* Captain
was astonished by what now happened.

Parsons:

'The *Captain* has put her helm down,' called the signal-luff.
'Only in the wind,' said the vice-admiral, 'she will box off directly.'

The admiral was wrong, and Commodore Sir Horatio Nelson
went clean about, and dashed in among the Spanish van, totally
unsupported – conduct totally unprecedented, and only to be
justified by the most complete success with which it was crowned.[32]

Drinkwater:

In executing this bold and decisive manoeuvre, the Commodore
reached the sixth ship from the enemy's rear, which was the
Spanish Admiral's own ship, the *Santissima Trinidad*, of 136 guns,
a ship of four decks, and said to be the largest in the world.
Notwithstanding the inequality of force, the Commodore instantly
engaged the colossal opponent, and for a considerable time had
to contend not only with her, but with her seconds a-head
and a-stern, of three decks each. While he maintained this
unequal combat, which he viewed with admiration mixed with
anxiety, his friends were flying to his support; and the enemy's
attention was soon directed to the *Culloden*, Captain Troubridge,
and in a short time after to the *Blenheim*, of ninety guns,

Captain Frederick, who opportunely came to their assistance.

The intrepid conduct of the Commodore staggered the Spanish Admiral, who already appeared to waver in pursuing his intention of joining the ships cut off by the British fleet, when the *Culloden*'s arrival, and Captain Troubridge's spirited support of the *Captain*, together with the approach of the *Blenheim*, followed by Rear-Admiral Parker, with the *Prince George, Orion, Irresistible*, and *Diadem*, not far distant, determined the Spanish Admiral to change his design altogether, and to make the signal for the ships of his main body to haul their wind, and make sail on the larboard tack.

Advantage was now apparent in favour of the British squadron, and not a moment was lost in improving it. As the ships of Rear-Admiral Parker's division approached the enemy's ships, in support of the *Captain* and her seconds, the *Blenheim* and *Culloden*, the cannonade became more animated and impressive. The superiority of the British fire over that of the enemy, and its effects on the enemy's hulls and sails, were so evident that we in the frigate no longer hesitated to pronounce a glorious termination of the contest.

The British squadron at this time was formed in two divisions, both on the larboard tack; their situation was as follows: Rear-Admiral Parker, with the *Blenheim, Culloden, Prince George, Captain, Orion, Irresistible*, composed one division, which was engaged with the enemy's rear. Sir John Jervis, with the other division, consisting of the *Excellent, Victory, Barfleur, Namur, Egmont, Goliath*, and *Britannia*, was pressing forward in support of his advanced squadron, but had not yet approached the real scene of action.

The *Colossus* having, in the early part of the day, unfortunately lost her fore-yard and fore-top-sail-yard, was obliged, in consequence of these losses, to fall to leeward, and the *Minerve*'s signal was made to take her in tow, which was, however, handsomely declined by Captain Murray, when the *Minerve* had come within hail in execution of her orders.

While the British advanced division warmly pressed the enemy's centre and rear, the Admiral meditated, with his division, a co-operation, which must effectually compel some of them to surrender.

In the confusion of their retreat, several of the enemy's ships had doubled on each other, and in the rear they were three or four deep. It was, therefore, the British Admiral's design to reach the weathermost of these ships, then bear up, and rake them all in succession with the seven ships composing his division. His object afterwards was to pass on to the support of his van division, which, from the length of time they had been engaged, he judged must be in want of it. The casual position, however, of the rear ships of his van division prevented his executing this plan: the Admiral, therefore, ordered the *Excellent*, the leading ship of his own division, to bear up; and, with the *Victory*, he himself passed to leeward of the enemy's rearmost and leewardmost ships, which, though almost silenced in their fire, continued obstinately to resist the animated attacks of all their opponents.[10]

Captain of the 74-gun Excellent was Cuthbert Collingwood, aged 49, but 'Old Cuddy' to his men. He was to be Nelson's second in command at the Battle of Trafalgar. Off Cape St Vincent he gained the recognition withheld from him by Howe following the 'Glorious First of June'.

The truth is, we did not proceed on any system of tactics [Collingwood wrote after the battle]. In the beginning we were formed very close and pushed at them without knowing, through the thickness of the haze, with what part of the line we could fall in. When they were divided, and the lesser part driven to leeward, the Admiral wisely abandoned them, made the signal to tack, and afterwards stuck to the larger divisions of the fleet, which was to windward, and could not be joined by the lee division in a short time. After this we had neither order nor signals, for the Admiral was so satisfied with the impetuosity of the attack made by the ships ahead of him that he let us alone.

The first ship we engaged was the *San Salvador del Mundo*, of 112 guns, a first rate; we were not further from her when we began than the length of our garden. Her colours soon came down, and her fire ceased. I hailed and asked if they surrendered; and when from signs made by a man who stood by the colours I understood they had, I left her to be taken possession of by somebody behind, and made sail for the next, but was very much surprised on looking back to find her colours up again, and the battle recommenced.

We very soon came up with the next, the *San Ysidro*, 74 guns, so close alongside that a man might jump from one ship to the other. Our fire carried all before it; and in ten minutes she hauled down her colours; but I had been deceived once, and obliged this fellow to hoist English colours before I left him, and made a signal for somebody behind to board him, when the Admiral ordered the *Lively* frigate to take charge of him.

Then making all sail, passing between our line and the enemy, we came up with the *San Nicolas*, of 80 guns, which happened at the time to be abreast of the *San Josef*, of 112 guns; we did not touch sides, but you could not put a bodkin between us, so that our shot passed through both ships, and in attempting to extricate themselves they got on board each other. My good friend, the Commodore, had been long engaged with these ships, and I came happily to his relief, for he was dreadfully mauled. Having engaged them until their fire ceased on me, though their colours were not down, I went on to the *Santissima Trinidad*, of 136 guns on four complete decks – such a ship as I never saw before. By this time our masts, sails and rigging were so much shot about that we could not get so near to her as I would have been; but near enough to receive much injury from her, both in my men and ship. We were engaged an hour with this ship, and trimmed her well; she was a complete wreck.[7]

Drinkwater:

Meanwhile, Sir John Jervis, disappointed in his plan of raking the enemy's rear ships, and having directed the *Excellent* to bear up, ordered the *Victory* to be placed on the leequarter of the rearmost ship of the enemy, a three-decker [the *Salvador del Mundo*], and having, by signal, ordered the *Irresistible* and *Diadem* to suspend their firing, threw into the three-decker so powerful a discharge, that her commander, seeing the *Barfleur*, carrying Vice-Admiral the Hon. W. Waldegrave's flag, ready to second the *Victory*, thought proper to strike to the British chief.[10]

As Jervis had taken the Victory *behind the Spanish weather division, a marine standing near the Admiral had his head carried away by a cannon ball and the Admiral was drenched by blood and brains. He wiped the blood from his face and called for an orange, which a midshipman hurriedly brought.*

Midshipman Parsons, in the Barfleur, *was also busy with oranges:*

After losing sight for some time of the little *Captain* among the leviathans of Spain, one of them, by some chance, appeared close under our stern; just as I had applied one of my select store of oranges to my mouth, she opened an ill-directed fire, apparently into the admiral's stern-galley, that I was viewing her from. The first bang caused a cessation of my labours, the second made me drop a remarkably fine Maltese orange, which rolled away and was no more seen, and the third made me close my commanders on the quarter-deck, bearing to each an orange.

An opening in the Spanish forest now showed the *Captain* on board of two Spanish ships, large enough to hoist her in, and to our astonishment and joy, a tattered Union Jack fluttered above their sweeping ensigns. The commodore had made a bridge of one, to capture the other, and both were prizes to the *Captain*, Sir Horatio Nelson.

At this time, the fleets being much intermingled, Sir John bore up in the *Victory* to rake the *Salvador del Mundo*, who carried a rear-admiral's flag, and had been roughly used by the *Excellent*, which had passed on to assist the *Orion*, engaged by the *Santissima Trinidad*. What a smashing broadside was sent into the unfortunate Spaniard's stern by the *Victory*! and before she could digest such a dose, we delivered another, which caused the Spanish flag to be quickly lowered, leaving our following friend to take possession of her.

When the British squadron passed through the Spanish fleet, they cut out eight ships of the line, who then tacked and kept hovering to windward of their distressed friends. The rear division now perceived the imminent peril of their commander-in-chief, who was dismasted and very hard pressed; indeed, it was roundly asserted that he struck his colours, and re-hoisted them on the rear division bearing down to his succour. The *Conde de Regla*, who led this division, ranging up alongside of His Majesty's ship *Britannia*, received one of the most destructive broadsides, and hauled her wind in a great hurry, taking no further part in the action.[32]

Nelson's account of his part in the action was as follows:

About one p.m., the *Captain* having passed the sternmost of the enemy's ships, which formed their van, consisting of seventeen sail of the line, and perceiving the Spanish fleet to bear up before the wind, evidently with the intention of forming their line, going large – joining their separated division – or flying from us; to prevent either of their schemes from taking effect, I ordered the ship to be wore, and passing between the *Diadem* and *Excellent*, at ten minutes past one o'clock, I was in close action with their van, and, of course, leewardmost of the Spanish fleet. The ships which I know were the *Santa Trinidad*, *San Josef*, *Salvador del Mundo*, *San Nicolas*, *San Ysidro*, another first-rate, and seventy-four, names not known. I was immediately joined and most nobly supported by the *Culloden*, Captain Troubridge.

The Spanish fleet, from not wishing, I suppose, to have a decisive battle, hauled to the wind on the larboard tack, which brought the ships above mentioned to be the leewardmost ships in their fleet. For an hour the *Culloden* and *Captain* supported this apparently, but not in reality, unequal contest, when the *Blenheim*, passing to windward of us and ahead, eased us a little.

By this time the *Salvador del Mundo* and *San Ysidro* dropped astern, and were fired into in a masterly style by the *Excellent*, Captain Collingwood, who compelled them to hoist English colours, when, disdaining the parade of taking possession of beaten enemies, he most gallantly pushed up to save his old friend and messmate, who was to appearance in a critical condition: the *Blenheim* having fallen to leeward, and the *Culloden* crippled and astern, the *Captain* at this time being actually fired upon by three first-rates and the *San Nicolas* and a seventy-four, and about pistol-shot distance of the *San Nicolas*. The *Excellent* ranged up with every sail set, and hauling up his mainsail just astern, passed within ten feet of the *San Nicolas*, giving her a most awful and tremendous fire. The *San Nicolas* luffing up, the *San Josef* fell on board her, and the *Excellent* passing on for the *Santa Trinidad*, the *Captain* resumed her situation abreast of them, close alongside.

At this time, the *Captain* having lost her fore-topmast, not a sail, shroud, or rope standing, the wheel shot away, and incapable of further service in the line or in chase, I directed Captain Miller to put the helm a-starboard, and calling for the boarders, ordered them to board.

The soldiers of the 69th Regiment, with an alacrity which will ever do them credit, with Lieutenant Pierson, of the same regiment, were amongst the foremost on this service. The first man who jumped into the enemy's mizen-chains was Captain Berry, late my First-Lieutenant. He was supported from our spritsail-yard; and a soldier of the 69th Regiment having broke the upper quarter-gallery window, jumped in, followed by myself and others, as fast as possible. I found the cabin doors fastened, and the Spanish officers fired their pistols at us through the windows, but having broke open the doors, the soldiers fired, and the Spanish Brigadier (Commodore, with a distinguishing pendant) fell as retreating to the quarter-deck. Having pushed on the quarter-deck, I found Captain Berry in possession of the poop, and the Spanish Ensign hauling down. The *San Josef* at this moment fired muskets and pistols from the Admiral's stern-gallery on us. Our seamen by this time were in full possession of every part: about seven of my men were killed, and some few wounded, and about twenty Spaniards.

Having placed sentinels at the different ladders, and ordered Captain Miller to push more men into the *San Nicolas*, I directed my brave fellows to board the first-rate, which was done in a moment. When I got into her main-chains, a Spanish officer came upon the quarter-deck rail, without arms, and said the ship had surrendered. From this welcome information, it was not long before I was on the quarter-deck, when the Spanish captain, with a bended knee, presented me his sword, and told me the Admiral was

KEY
- British Fleet
- Spanish Fleet

Fig. 1. Plan of the Battle of St Vincent at 13.00 hours.

dying with his wound below. I gave him my hand, and desired him to call to his officers and ship's company that the ship had surrendered, which he did; and on the quarter-deck of a Spanish first-rate, extravagant as the story may seem, did I receive the swords of the vanquished Spaniards, which as I received I gave to William Fearney, one of my bargemen, who placed them, with the greatest sang-froid, under his arm. I was surrounded by Captain Berry, Lieutenant Pierson, 69th Regiment, John Sykes, John Thompson, Francis Cook, and William Fearney, all old Agamemnons, and several other brave men, seamen and soldiers.

Thus fell these ships. The *Victory* passing saluted us with three cheers, as did every ship in the fleet.

The *Minerve* sent a boat for me, and I hoisted my pendant on board her, directing Captain Cockburn to put me on board the first uninjured ship of the line, which was done; and I hoisted my pendant in the *Irresistible*, but the day was too far advanced to venture on taking possession of the *Santa Trinidad*, although she had long ceased to resist, as it must have brought on a night action with a still very superior fleet.

. . . There is a saying in the Fleet too flattering for me to omit telling – viz., 'Nelson's Patent Bridge for boarding First-Rates,' alluding to my passing over an enemy's 80-gun ship.[28]

Nelson's daring enterprise with the Captain *was to put in the shade the exploits of the other British ships that day. But Cordova, the Spanish Commander-in-Chief, in his despatch, put down his defeat to the attack on his main body from the* Culloden *and the other ships of the van who had tacked and engaged the enemy with crippling success for an hour before the* Captain *entered the battle so dramatically.*

So soon as their headmost ship had passed athwart our stern [writes Cordova], she tacked, followed by five or six others passing our line to windward; the remaining ten ships, that were before on our larboard side, then bore up at the same time, and passed through our line in different positions, and consequently remained on the other tack fighting us in great order, with a heavy and well-directed fire: this manoeuvre decided the action in their favour.

I did not fail to guard against this from the commencement, and anticipated it by ordering the ships ahead to tack and gain the enemy's rear to leeward; and if the commanders of the *Principe*, *Regla*, *Oriente*, and *Firme* had availed themselves of the opportunity to join six or eight ships of the van, they would have placed the enemy between two fires, and terminated the action in a very different manner.

Although the *Principe* and *Regla* were not able to fall into the rear of our line, they notwithstanding did their utmost from their situation, engaging the enemy at the time of passing our line, till they had obtained the weather gage.

The attack of the enemy was now principally on the *Trinidad*, which, from the crippled situation of her mast and rigging, fell to leeward. By word of mouth, and by signals, the *Salvador*, *San Josef*, *Soberano*, and *San Nicolas* were ordered to shorten sail, and to form in our rear, which they executed with celerity, maintaining a severe action. The van continually remaining to windward, at two I made them a signal to shorten sail, and bear down for a general attack.

The *Mexicano* formed upon our bow about three in the afternoon, and engaged the foremost ship of the enemy's line; they now for the remainder of the day fixed their whole attention against the *San Josef*, *Mexicano*, *San Nicolas*, and *San Ysidro*, which were the only ships to bear the principal and hottest part of the action against the whole enemy's squadron.

In this situation it would have been highly expedient that our centre and van should have come to our support, but it was out of my power to intimate to them the necessity of this movement, the ships being in want of masts, rigging, and every necessary for making signals.

I cannot refrain from giving due praise to the valour of the above-mentioned ships formed at my stern, and expressing the gallant manner in which they behaved during the engagement: but at length, being dismasted and destroyed, some struck, and others left the action. The *Trinidad* was attacked the whole afternoon by a three-decker, and three ships of 74-guns, that raked her fore and aft at pistol-shot; and notwithstanding her having upwards of two hundred men killed and wounded, she still continued the action for a full hour longer.

Such was the dreadful situation of the *Trinidad* at six o'clock, after an uninterrupted engagement, when the *San Pablo* and *Pelayo*, that in the morning had been detached by my orders, and crowded every sail from the moment of observing the action, now reached the squadron.

The reinforcement of these two ships happened at the opportune junction of the *Conde de Regla*; the *Principe* arrived shortly after, and the enemy, observing our van standing towards them, immediately retired together, covering the captured ships *San Josef*, *Salvador*, *San Ysidro*, and *San Nicolas*.[8]

Midshipman Parsons, the Barfleur:

The time now nearly five p.m., and two first-rates and two second-rates showed the gay Union of England fluttering over the ensign of Spain. Our prizes and disabled ships had fallen to leeward, and as the day was closing, Sir John, who must have been amazed at his own success, made the signal for the fleet to re-form the line of battle to leeward, and bore up in the *Victory* to close them, and formed his line just to windward of his prizes, between them and the Spanish fleet, which still remained in the greatest disorder, their commander-in-chief, in the *Santissima*, with only her mainmast and mainyard standing. I believe the slaughter on board her so unprecedented that Don Cordova, on shifting his flag, stated he had left four hundred of his men dead on her decks.[32]

The British ships, too, had taken a battering: the rigging of most of them was severely damaged, little ammunition remained, and the crews were nearly exhausted after a full day's battle.

Veteran mariner John Nicol tells how it was on the Goliath:

During the action, my situation was not one of danger, but most wounding to my feelings, and trying to my patience. I was stationed in the after magazine, serving powder from the screen, and could see nothing; but I could feel every shot that struck the *Goliath*; and the cries and groans of the wounded were most distressing, as there was only the thickness of the blankets of the screen between me and them.

Busy as I was the time hung upon me with a dreary weight. Not a soul spoke to me but the master-at-arms, as he went his rounds to inquire if all was safe. No sick person ever longed more for his physician than I for the voice of the master-at-arms. The surgeon's-mate, at the commencement of the action, spoke a little; but his hands were soon too full of his own affairs. Those who were carrying ran like wild creatures, and scarce opened their lips. I would far rather have been on the decks, amid the bustle, for there the time flew on eagle's wings.

The *Goliath* was sore beset; for some time she had two three-deckers upon her. The men stood to their guns as cool as if they had been exercising. The Admiral ordered the *Britannia* to our assistance. 'Iron-sides', with her forty-twos, soon made them sheer off.

Towards the close of the action, the men were very weary. One lad put his head out of the port-hole, saying, 'Damn them, are they not going to strike yet?' For us to strike was out of the question.

At length the roar of the guns ceased, and I came on deck to see the effects of a great sea engagement; but such a scene of blood and desolation I want words to express.

The fleet was in such a shattered situation, we lay twenty-four hours in sight of them, repairing our rigging. It is after the action the disagreeable part commences; the crews are wrought to the utmost of their strength; for days they have no remission of their toil; repairing the rigging and other parts injured in the action; their spirits are broke by fatigue. They have no leisure to talk of the battle; and, when the usual round of duty returns, we do not choose to revert to a disagreeable subject. Who can speak of what he did, when all did their utmost? [30]

Answer: an ambitious commodore who, whatever his virtues, did not number modesty among them at this stage in his naval career. At the first opportunity he described his unorthodox capture of two

Spanish ships in an account entitled 'A Few Remarks Relative to Myself in the Captain, *in which my pendant was flying on the most glorious Valentine's Day, 1797', on which we have drawn, pages 38–41. If taking* Captain *out of line had not been crowned with dramatic success, one wonders what reception Nelson would have had from Sir John Jervis. But, as it was:*

At dusk, I went on board the *Victory*, when the Admiral received me on the quarter-deck, and having embraced me, said he could not sufficiently thank me, and used every kind expression which could not fail to make me happy.[28]

Nelson does not mention that on the morning of the 15th he went on board the frigate Lively, *hoping to see Sir Gilbert Elliot, whom he knew would be the first man home to London with the story of the battle. Sir Gilbert had gone over to the* Victory, *but Nelson gave an enthusiastic account of his part in the battle to Colonel Drinkwater, whose* Narrative of the Battle of St Vincent *did more than anything to publicize Nelson's exploits on St Valentine's Day (he refers to Nelson as 'the intrepid Commodore', 'the Hero', etc.):*

I made pencil notes on a scrap of paper I found at hand; and these communications from my gallant friend were the more valuable from their being made before he had seen any other officer of the fleet, except Captain G. Martin, of the *Irresistible*, to which ship he had repaired for refreshment and repose, until the *Captain*, his own ship, almost a wreck in her rigging, etc., could be put into manageable order.

Towards the conclusion of this interesting interview, I repeated my cordial felicitations at his personal safety, after such very perilous achievements. I then adverted to the honours that must attend such distinguished services. 'The Admiral', I observed, 'of course will be made a peer, and his seconds in command noticed accordingly. As for you, Commodore,' I continued, 'they will make you a baronet.' The word was scarcely uttered, when placing his hand on my arm, and looking at me most expressively in the face, he said, 'No, no: if they want to mark my services, it must not be in that manner.' – 'Oh!' said I, interrupting him, 'you wish to be made a Knight of the Bath,' for I could not imagine that his amibition, at that time, led him to expect a peerage. My supposition proved to be correct, for he instantly answered me, 'Yes; if my services have been of any value, let them be noticed in a way that the public may know me – or them.'[10]

Nelson knew that Drinkwater's notes would be passed on to Sir Gilbert Elliot, with the result he expected: the Order of the Bath and promotion to Rear-Admiral. A peerage had been agreed for Jervis shortly before the battle, and he now became Earl of St Vincent.

No honours awaited Admiral José de Cordova, who was arrested as soon as the Santissima Trinidad* *made it to Cadiz. Still with superior strength to the British, he had pondered the possibility of renewing the engagement at daylight on the 15th. Young Midshipman Parsons had the idea that an accident on board the* Barfleur *at least in part deterred such a move by the enemy:*

Our fleet, during the night (of the 14th/15th), which was fine, repaired damages and shifted prisoners, both fleets lying to, with a prospect of renewing the fight at daylight. At dawn of day, the Spaniards, exasperated at their unexpected defeat and heavy losses, made a demonstration of fight, by forming the line of battle, and placing their heads towards us, bringing up with them a very light breeze. An affirmative to the question, 'Are you ready to renew the action?' flew at the masthead of each of our ships of the line, as the leeward ones, mostly disabled, were towed into the British line of battle.

At this moment a violent explosion from our lower-deck, with the hasty flight of the port, part of the side, and a round shot of thirty-two pounds, through the air, caused great excitement; and the cry of fire ensuing, caused some confusion in the *Barfleur*. This was speedily got under, and our captain made his appearance on the quarter-deck completely drenched, and proceeded to inquire into the late alarming occurrence.

The men had slept at quarters, and one of them was soundly sleeping on the breech of a lower-deck gun that was housed. A

---

* This huge ship had stuck to the *Orion*, commanded by Sir James Saumarez, then resumed Spanish colours. She was taken and sunk at the Battle of Trafalgar.

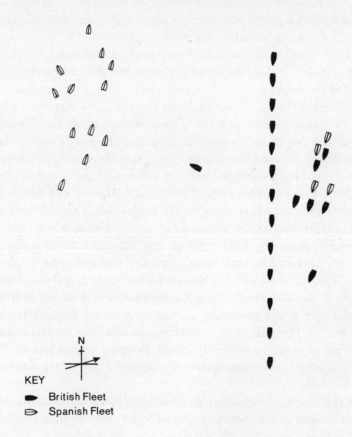

KEY
- British Fleet
- Spanish Fleet

Fig. 2. Plan of the Battle of St Vincent at 17.00 hours.

waister from the sister-kingdom, rather raw in the service, possessed of an inquiring mind, was at a loss to determine how pulling a string affixed to the lock could cause such a thundering noise; in his philosophical experiment he had placed the lock on full cock, gave a gentle pull with the aforesaid string, fired the gun, killed the sleeper, smashed his foot to pieces by the recoil, and stood transfixed with horror and pain at the success of his experiment. The loss of his foot saved his back, and the carpenters soon repaired the damage.

Whether the noise of our shot was the cause, or that the better part of valour influenced the Dons, they hauled their wind, which now began to freshen, and increased their distance. By signal from the commander-in-chief, the British fleet hoisted Spanish colours, in compliment to Don something* – whose flag had been flying on board the *Salvador del Mundo*, and who was now dying of wounds received in the action. Whether this refined compliment cheered his moments of agony I cannot say, but it received its reward by a rich Spanish ship running into the midst of us, being bothered by both fleets appearing with the same colours.

Sir John, satisfied with the honour he had gained, and entertaining a well-founded dread of the Toulon fleet, which he would have found a very rough customer, shaped a course for Lagos Bay, on the coast of Portugal, with the prizes in tow; the Spanish fleet following us, though evidently afraid to come within gunshot.[32]

In Lagos Bay the elements nearly succeeded where the Spanish fleet had failed.

On the following morning we anchored in battle order across this open bay, and in the evening a gale of wind came in from the sea, and the fleet was in terrible jeopardy, most of the ships with their sheet anchor down, and some with their spare one. In the *Barfleur* we were pitching bows under, with three anchors ahead; one mile astern of us extended a reef of rocks, on which the sea broke frightfully, and through which there appeared no opening; half a

---

* Admiral F. J. Winthuysen, wounded fatally on board the *San Josef*. His sword was presented by Nelson to the city of Norwich.

mile within them lay a populous village of fishermen, and as they expected a God-send by the wreck of the whole fleet, they had gone through the trouble of collecting wood and burning fires through the night. Young as I was, I retain a strong recollection of this dark and dreadful night.

'Ship ahead driving,' called the forecastle lieutenant.

'God help us!' I heard the captain piously ejaculate. 'Lower-deck there, stand by, to veer on three cables at the same time – place the helm hard a starboard' – and the commander-in-chief, in his gallant and noble ship, the *Victory*, passed our starboard side close, driving fast upon the rocks to leeward, which shook off the heavy sea, throwing its white spray to the clouds. There was an agonized cry of horror, and 'O God! save her!' as this beautiful fabric hastened on destruction. We heard her last effort, as her spare anchor flashed in the briny flood, and, thank God, she brought up with four anchors a-head.

Never shall I forget the sight, as I caused our stern and top lanterns to be relighted. The roaring of the wind and rain, the bellowing noise of the officers' trumpets, the booming of the numerous guns of distress, the roar of the breakers so near us astern, and the ghastly reflection of the surf and fires ashore – all, all are imprinted on my memory, to the year in which I write.[32]

Cadiz and Santa Cruz

July 1797

Mortals cannot command success.
Earl St Vincent.

Shortly after the triumph off Cape St Vincent came the disastrous raid on Santa Cruz, in which Nelson lost his right arm.

After the action of St Valentine's Day, Nelson's wife had implored:

I sincerely hope, my dear husband, that all these wonderful and desperate actions – such as boarding ships – you will leave to others. With the protection of a Supreme Being, you have acquired a character or name which, all heads agree, cannot be greater; therefore, rest satisfied.[6]

It was not in Nelson's nature to rest satisfied. A few months later he was putting his life in danger again, at Cadiz and at Santa Cruz.

Towards the end of May, Nelson – newly appointed a Rear-Admiral of the Blue – hoisted his flag in the Theseus *under Captain Ralph Miller, and was given command of the inshore squadron off Cadiz. The* Theseus *was one of the ships touched by the mutinies in home waters, but the stabilizing influence of a popular captain and admiral was soon apparent.*

Nelson to Fanny, 15th June:

A few nights ago a Paper was dropped on the quarter-deck, of which this is a copy: – 'Success attend Admiral Nelson! God bless Captain Miller! We thank them for the officers they have placed over us. We are happy and comfortable, and will shed every drop of blood in our veins to support them, and the name of the *Theseus* shall be immortalized as high as the *Captain*'s. SHIP'S COMPANY.'[6]

Nelson organized a bombardment of the town of Cadiz on 3rd July, placing his life in danger. His barge was engaged by a Spanish gunboat.

From the Sketch of My Life:

I was boarded in my barge with its common crew of ten men, cockswain, Captain Fremantle, and myself, by the commander of the gunboats. The Spanish barge rowed twenty-six oars, besides officers, thirty in the whole; this was a service hand-to-hand with swords, in which my cockswain, John Sykes (now no more), saved twice my life. Eighteen of the Spaniards being killed and several wounded, we succeeded in taking their commander.[29]

But not without a desperate struggle. An anonymous eye-witness tells how close Nelson came to being killed:

The commandant of the Spanish, a gallant fellow, Don Miguel Tyrason, singled out the Admiral's barge; in which was John Sykes, as gallant a sailor as ever took up slops from a purser, or shared his grog with his mess-mates. Don Miguel ordered his boat to be placed alongside of ours; and, as you may suppose, we did not object to the meeting, although she was a powerful craft.

Don Miguel led his men bravely, and to give them the credit they deserve, they were worthy of such a gallant commander, and of the honour of being killed by us.

Nelson parried a blow which would have saved him from being at the Nile, and Fremantle [Captain Thomas Fremantle of the *Seahorse*] fought like himself, fore and aft, both boats. It was a desperate struggle, and once we were nearly carried.

John Sykes was close to Nelson on his left hand, and he seemed more concerned for the Admiral's life than his own: he hardly ever struck a blow but to save his gallant officer. Twice he parried blows that must have been fatal to Nelson; for Sykes was a man whose coolness gave him full scope for the Science at Single Stick, and who never knew what fear was, any more than his Admiral. It was cut, thrust, fire, and no load again – we had no time for that. The Spaniards fought like devils, and seemed resolved to win from the Admiral the laurels of his former victory; they appeared to know him, and directed their particular attack towards the officers.

Twice had Sykes saved him; and now he saw a blow descending which would have severed the head of Nelson. In that second of thought which a cool man possesses, Sykes saw that he could not ward the blow with his cutlass; the situation of the Spaniard rendered it impossible. He saw the danger; that moment expired, and Nelson would have been a corpse: but Sykes saved him – he interposed his own hand!

We all saw it – we were witnesses to the gallant deed, and we gave in revenge one cheer and one tremendous rally. Eighteen of the Spaniards were killed, and we boarded and carried her; there not being one man left on board who was not either dead or wounded.

'Sykes,' said Nelson as he caught the gallant fellow in his arms, 'I cannot forget this.' But my wounded shipmate only looked him in the face, and smiled, as he said: 'Thank God, Sir, you are safe.'[6]

Sykes received a gunner's warrant, but a year later was killed by a relatively common occurrence – a cannon bursting.

Cadiz was bombarded a second time on the 5th.

On their way home from America Spanish treasure ships, and others carrying rich cargoes, were in the habit of calling at Santa Cruz on the island of Tenerife. Nelson was fired with the idea of taking the port and any ships in it. St Vincent finally agreed, and on 15th July Nelson was detached with a squadron of four line-of-battle ships, three frigates, and a cutter, which reached Tenerife on the 21st.

The first attempt at a landing was prevented by heavy surf and troublesome inshore currents, and a further attempt, under Captain Troubridge, also failed. Though the Spanish garrison was by now fully alerted, Nelson decided upon a night attack, led by himself.

He wrote to St Vincent on the 24th:

Theseus, off Santa Cruz,
July 24th: 8 p.m.

My dear Sir,

I shall not enter on the subject while we are not in possession of Santa Cruz; your partiality will give me credit that all has hitherto been done which was possible, but without effect. This night, I, humble as I am, command the whole, destined to land under the batteries of the Town, and tomorrow my head will probably be crowned with either laurel or cypress. I have only to recommend Josiah Nisbet to you and my Country. With every affectionate wish for your health, and every blessing in the world, believe me your most faithful

Horatio Nelson.

The Duke of Clarence, should I fall, in the service of my King and Country, will, I am confident, take a lively interest for my son-in-law, on his name being mentioned.[6]

It was the last letter Nelson wrote with his right hand.

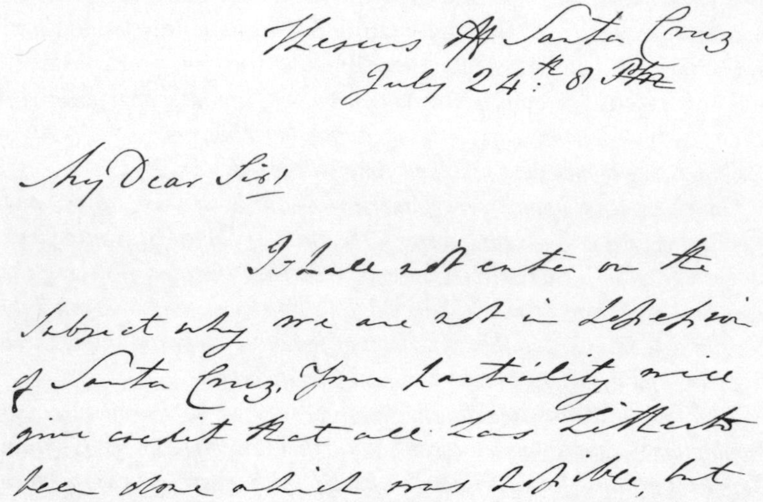

Fig. 3. Letter written by Nelson to his Commander-in-Chief, Sir John Jervis, shortly before losing his right arm.

He tried, unsuccessfully, to dissuade Josiah Nisbet from going on the raid, fearing that Fanny might lose husband and son in one night. And before setting out, he made a will.

A heavy sea was running, and some boats never reached shore. About 1.00 a.m. the raid was spotted, and the Spaniards opened fire with cannons and muskets. Nelson's party landed on the harbour mole, and took it after a fierce fight. But, in the end, the landing parties could not take the strongly-defended port, and British losses were high.

Nelson's right arm was shattered by a grapeshot as he was in the act of drawing his sword and about to step ashore. He exclaimed: 'I am a dead man!', and was laid, white-faced and bleeding, in the bottom of the boat, and rowed back to the Theseus.

On board was a young midshipman, William Hoste, who had gone to sea under Nelson's protection, and wrote home:

About five, came to an anchor to the eastward of the town, in company with the *Culloden, Zealous*, and *Leander* line of battle ships, and *Seahorse, Terpsichore*, and *Emerald* frigates, cutter and gunboats standing towards the town. At half-past seven the mortar-boat began to throw shells into the town. At half-past ten the marines and seamen from the different ships put off and began to row towards the mole head, under the command of our brave admiral.

At one a.m. commenced one of the heaviest cannonading I ever was witness to from the town upon our boats, likewise a heavy fire of musketry, which continued without intermission for the space of four hours.

At two, Admiral Nelson returned on board, being dreadfully wounded in the right arm with a grapeshot. I leave you to judge of my situation when I beheld our boat approach with him, whom I may say has been a second father to me, his right arm dangling by his side, and with a spirit that astonished everyone, told the surgeon to get his instruments ready, for he knew that he must lose his arm, and the sooner it was off the better.

He underwent the amputation with the same firmness and courage that have always marked his character.[16]

Nelson's surgeon's report:
Medical Journal of H.M.S. *Theseus:*
Kept by Thomas Eshelby, Surgeon.
Date: 1797, July 25.
Patient: Admiral Nelson.
Remarks: Compound fracture of the right arm by a musket ball
   passing through a little above the elbow, an artery divided.
   The arm was immediately amputated and the following given
   him:
Opii gr. ii.ft.Pil.statim.s.
1797, July 26. Rested pretty well and quite easy. Tea, soup, and
   sago. Lemonade and Tamarind drink.[34]

*Lloyd's List, 6 February 1933, repeated a story carried in the
French naval journal,* Le Yacht, *that Nelson's arm was kept behind
the altar at the cathedral of Las Palmas, Grand Canary, to the great
benefit of the collecting boxes in that edifice.*

*The Santa Cruz expedition was a tragic failure, though a truce
was arranged and Nelson and the Governor exchanged courteous
letters and gifts.*

*Nelson's spirits were at their lowest when he wrote an unsteady
left-handed letter to his Commander-in-Chief:*

My dear sir,

I am become a burthen to my friends, and useless to my
Country; but by my letter wrote the 24th, you will perceive my
anxiety for the promotion of my son-in-law, Josiah Nisbet. When
I leave your command, I become dead to the world; I go hence,
and am no more seen. If from poor Bowen's [Captain Richard
Bowen of the *Terpsichore*, killed in the action] loss, you think it
proper to oblige me, I rest confident you will do it; the boy is
under obligations to me, but he repaid me by bringing me from
the Mole of Santa Cruz. I hope you will be able to give me a
frigate, to convey the remains of my carcase to England. God bless
you, my dear sir, and believe me, your most obliged and faithful,

Horatio Nelson.
You will excuse my scrawl, considering it is my first attempt.[6]

But, on his return to the Mediterranean Fleet, Nelson regained his confidence. Sir John Jervis put out of mind the self-pitying letter he had received and consoled the little Admiral with: 'Mortals cannot command success.'

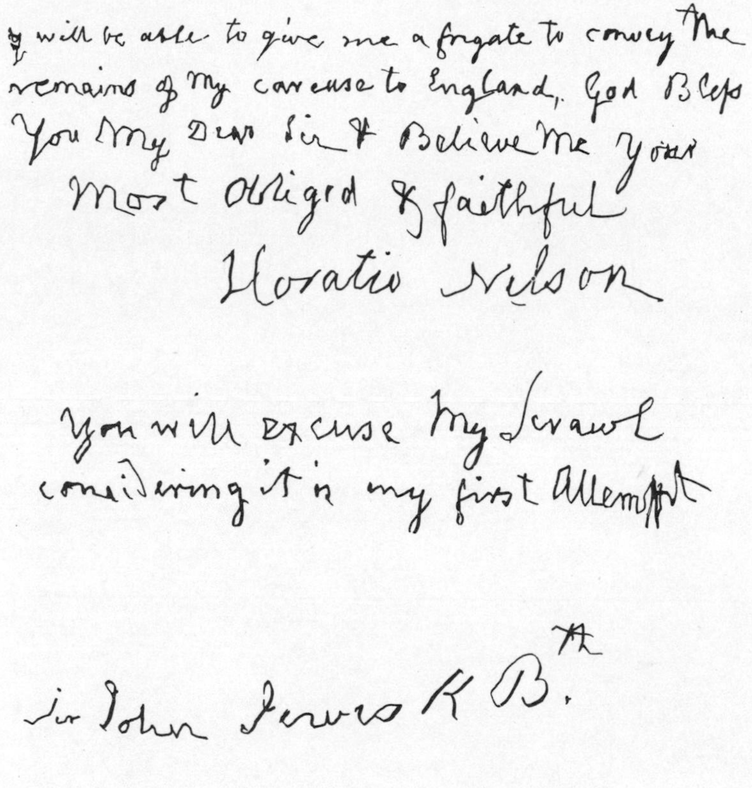

y will be able to give me a frigate to convey the remains of my carcase to England, God Bless You My Dear Sir & Believe Me your Most Obliged & faithful

Horatio Nelson

You will excuse My Scrawl considering it is my first Attempt

Sir John Jervis K B.

Fig. 4. Letter written by Nelson to Sir John Jervis shortly after losing his right arm.

The Battle of the Nile

1 August 1798

The glorious victory of the first of August is
like the Church of St Peter's at Rome. It
strikes you at first sight from its magnitude,
but the more you examine its dimensions and
details the more wonderful it appears.
Sir William Hamilton.

British Ships at the Battle of the Nile

(Key numbers refer to fig. 5)

Vanguard (6)	74 guns	Rear-Admiral Sir H. Nelson
		Captain Edward Berry
Orion (3)	74 guns	Captain Sir James Saumarez
Culloden (4)	74 guns	Captain Thomas Troubridge
Bellerophon (8)	74 guns	Captain Henry Darby
Minotaur (7)	74 guns	Captain Thomas Louis
Defence (9)	74 guns	Captain William Peyton
Alexander (11)	74 guns	Captain Alexander Ball
Zealous (2)	74 guns	Captain Samuel Hood
Audacious (4)	74 guns	Captain Davidge Gould
Goliath (1)	74 guns	Captain Thomas Foley
Theseus (5)	74 guns	Captain Ralph Miller
Majestic (10)	74 guns	Captain George Westcott
Swiftsure (12)	74 guns	Captain Benjamin Hallowell
Leander (13)	50 guns	Captain Thomas Thompson
Mutine (brig.) (15)	18 guns	Captain Thomas Masterman Hardy

French Ships at the Battle of the Nile

(Key numbers refer to fig. 5)

L'Orient (22) (burnt)	120 guns	Admiral F. Brueys, Commander-in-Chief
		Admiral H. Ganteaume, Chief of Staff
		Captain Casabianca
Le Franklin (21) (taken)	80 guns	First Contre Admiral Blanquet (wounded)
		Captain Gillet (wounded)
Le Guillaume Tell (26) (escaped)	80 guns	Second Contre Admiral Villeneuve
		Captain Saumer
Le Tonnant (23) (taken)	80 guns	Captain Dupetit-Thouars (killed)
Le Guerrier (16) (taken)	74 guns	Captain Trulet, Sen.
Le Timoléon (25) (burnt)	74 guns	Captain Trulet, Jun.
Le Conquérant (17) (taken)	74 guns	Captain Dalbarade (wounded)
Le Spartiate (18) (taken)	74 guns	Captain Emereau (wounded)
L'Aquilon (19) (taken)	74 guns	Captain Thevenard (killed)
Le Peuple Souverain (20)	74 guns	Captain Raccord (wounded)
L'Heureux (24) (taken)	74 guns	Captain Étienne (wounded)
Le Mercure (27) (taken)	74 guns	Captain Cambon (wounded)
Le Généreux (28) (escaped)	74 guns	Captain Lejoille

FRIGATES

La Diane (31) (escaped)	48 guns	Admiral de Crepe
		Captain Soleil
La Justice (32) (escaped)	44 guns	Captain Villeneuve, Jun.
L'Artémise (30) (burnt)	36 guns	Captain Estandlet
La Sérieuse (29) (sunk)	36 guns	Captain Martin

Nelson returned to England in September 1797 to convalesce at Bath and London. The wound caused by the amputation of his arm was slow to heal; but by the spring of '98 he felt ready again for service at sea. His part in the Battle of St Vincent had earned him a knighthood and recognition as a brilliant sea-officer in official circles in London. The Battle of the Nile was to make him a national hero.

He was delighted when in the following April Lord Spencer, the First Lord, ordered him to hoist his flag on the 11-year-old Vanguard, a fast-sailing ship, of 74 guns, and join the Earl of St Vincent's fleet based on Portugal. This Nelson did, to soon find himself entrusted with an assignment of great importance.

When word reached England that France was preparing a large expedition from bases in the Mediterranean, it became imperative that the Royal Navy should again enter those waters. The First Lord wrote to St Vincent telling him to send a squadron into the Mediterranean, suggesting that if he did not command it personally he should put it 'under the command of Sir H. Nelson, whose acquaintance with that part of the world, as well as his activity and disposition, seem to qualify him in a peculiar manner for that service'. St Vincent had already done so before the letter was received, and Nelson, in the Vanguard, under Captain Berry, had set out with two other 74-gun ships, the Orion, Sir James Saumarez, and the Alexander, Captain Alexander Ball. Spencer had told St Vincent, 'The appearance of a British squadron in the Mediterranean is a condition on which the fate of Europe may at this moment be stated to depend.'

It was a heavy responsibility for a 39-year-old rear-admiral of twelve months' seniority and Nelson's first weeks in the Mediterranean were to prove unlucky and nerve-fraying. There was an early misfortune. The Vanguard was dismasted in a storm and might have been wrecked had not the Alexander taken her in tow. The situation was so perilous that at one point Nelson hailed Ball to cast off. Ball

refused and earned Nelson's undying gratitude by bringing the
Vanguard *in safely to a bay in the island of St Peter's, off Sardinia.*
 Nelson was humbled by the experience, and wrote to his wife on
24th May:

I ought not to call what has happened to the *Vanguard* by the
cold name of accident; I believe firmly that it was the Almighty's
goodness to check my consummate vanity. I hope it has made me a
better officer, as I feel confident that it has made me a better man.

Figure to yourself a vain man on Sunday evening at sunset
walking in his cabin with a squadron about him who looked up to
their Chief to lead them to glory and in whom the Chief placed the
firmest reliance that the proudest ships in equal numbers belonging
to France would have bowed their flags . . . . Figure to yourself
this proud conceited man, when the sun rose on Monday morning,
his ship dismasted, his fleet dispersed and himself in such peril
that the meanest frigate out of France would have been a very
unwelcome guest. But it has pleased Almighty God to bring us
into a safe port where altho' we are refused the rights of humanity,
yet the *Vanguard* will in two days get to sea again, as an Englishman of War. The exertions of Sir James Saumarez and Captain
Ball have been wonderful and if the ship had been in England,
months would have been taken to send her back. Here my operations will not be delayed four days, and I shall join the rest of my
fleet on the rendezvous.

If this letter gets to you, be so good as to write a line to Lord
Spencer telling him that the *Vanguard* is fitted tolerably for sea,
and that what has happened will not retard my operations.[9]

And a week later to St Vincent:

My dear Lord,

My pride was too great for man, but I must trust my friends will
think I bore my chastisement like a man. It has pleased God to
assist me with His favour, and here I am again, off Toulon.[9]

While the Vanguard *was being repaired the squadron was power-
fully reinforced by the arrival of ten ships. Nelson had now a superb
fleet under his command, with captains who had mostly been in fleet*

actions. By order of seniority, Sir James Saumarez of the Orion *was second in command, and third in command the* Culloden's *Captain Thomas Troubridge. Saumarez had been in four fleet actions, including St Vincent, in which Troubridge had led the line. Both ships had figured in Howe's 'Glorious First of June', as had the* Audacious *under Captain Davidge Gould, the* Majestic, *Captain George Westcott, and the oldest of the ships, the* Defence, *launched in 1762. The* Goliath *had been at St Vincent, her present Captain, Thomas Foley, having served on the* Britannia *in that battle. Nelson's friend, Captain Ralph Miller, was with the* Theseus, *which had worn Nelson's flag at Tenerife. Also at Tenerife were the* Zealous, *Captain Samuel Hood, and the* Leander, *Captain Thomas Thompson. The* Minotaur *under Captain Thomas Louis was to serve at Trafalgar, where the* Swiftsure, *Captain Benjamin Hallowell, was destined to be retaken from the French. The squadron was completed by the brig* Mutine, *captured from the French at Santa Cruz the previous year and now commanded by Thomas Masterman Hardy. All the ships were of 74 guns, with the exceptions of the 50-gun* Leander *and the 18-gun* Mutine.*

On the day, 20th May, that Nelson had suffered the humiliation of the Vanguard's *near wreck, a massive French convoy had sailed from Toulon – 13 ships-of-the-line, 7 frigates, several gunboats, and 300 transports. The expedition was commanded by Napoleon Bonaparte, then aged 29. For eight weeks, to and fro in the Mediterranean, Nelson was to hunt the French Fleet. Luck was with Bonaparte.*

He landed at Malta, overcame token resistance from the ruling Knights of St John, abolished their Order, and set up a new governing body – all in a week. Then the armada set sail again, leaving a garrison on the island.

Nelson believed – correctly – that the French expedition was heading for Egypt with the intention of taking Alexandria, and then the whole of Egypt. His senior captains confirming his opinion, Nelson ordered the British squadron to set sail for Alexandria; they reached the port on 29th June, but found no French ships at anchor.

Dejected, Nelson resumed his Mediterranean search, complaining bitterly that 'the Devil's children have the Devil's luck'. He felt he must justify himself to his chief, writing to St Vincent:

I determined, with the opinions of those captains in whom I place great confidence, to go to Alexandria; and if that place, or any other part of Egypt was their destination, I hoped to arrive time enough to frustrate their plans. The only objection I can fancy to be stated is, 'You should not have gone such a long voyage without more certain information of the enemy's destination.' My answer is ready – who was I to get it from?

The governments of Naples and Sicily either knew not, or chose to keep me in ignorance. Was I to wait patiently till I heard certain accounts? If Egypt was their object, before I could hear of them they would have been in India. To do nothing, I felt, was disgraceful; therefore I made use of my understanding, and by it I ought to stand or fall. I am before your Lordship's judgment (which in the present case I feel is the tribunal of my country) and if, under all circumstances, it is decided that I am wrong, I ought, for the sake of our country, to be superseded.[27]

Nelson had no need, at that stage at any rate, to justify his going to Alexandria. The tone of the letter reveals the mental strain its writer was then undergoing. He confessed afterwards that these weeks of fruitless search for the French were among the most trying of his life. His nerves were frayed and his heart was given to sudden races at any startling sound. He was suffering the anguish of the born fighter tantalizingly deprived of a fight.

In a more spirited manner, he wrote St Vincent a few days later:

Your Lordship deprived yourself of frigates to make mine certainly the first squadron in the world, and I feel that I have zest and activity to do credit to your appointment, and yet to be unsuccessful hurts me most sensibly. But if they are above water I will find them out, and if possible bring them to battle.[27]

A break for Nelson came on 28th July. Troubridge took the Culloden *into the Gulf of Coron; he came out with a French wine brig in tow. The wine was welcome, but even more welcome the news Troubridge had received from the garrison's Turkish governor. The French armada had been sighted off the coast of Crete four weeks before . . .* sailing south-east. *Nelson, and his captains, had been right after all; their ill-luck had been to arrive at Alexandria ahead of the French, though barely so. They had, in fact, twice missed the French fleet by only a few hours. On the night of 22nd June, shortly after leaving Sicily, they had passed so close to the French armada that the latter had heard the British signal guns, causing Bonaparte to order a diversion along the coast of Crete. The second occasion was at Alexandria itself. On 29th June Nelson's squadron had scarcely left the port when the French convoy sailed into view of the Alexandrians.*

Nelson was thus denied the opportunity 'to try Bonaparte on a wind'. The Admiral had respect for the General as a land fighter; but as Commander of the Fleet . . .?

Bonaparte rapidly confirmed his military skill. Inside three weeks he took Alexandria, won the Battle of the Pyramids, and marched his victorious army into Cairo.

Acting immediately on the Turkish governor's information, Nelson and the men he called his 'band of brothers' reached Alexandria again on 1 August 1798:

Captain Samuel Hood of the Zealous:

At half-past ten *Alexander* made the signal for the land. At half-past eleven we saw it was Alexandria, and as we approached we could plainly discern there were many more vessels in the port than when we were there before, and the *Alexander* made the signal for six French ships of war lying in the port, and we soon discovered the enemy fleet had been here.

I immediately kept well to the eastward of the Admiral to try if I could make out anything at Aboukir, as did also the *Goliath*. At about half-past one the man at the masthead said he saw a sail and instantly a fleet at anchor. I sent a glass up and they told me there were sixteen or eighteen large ships – they thought sixteen of the line. I immediately made the signal to the Admiral, who instantly made all sail and the signal to prepare for battle.[15]

The honour of signalling sight of the enemy had nearly gone to the Goliath *and Captain Foley – as a disappointed Midshipman Elliot relates:*

I, as signal-midshipman, was sweeping round the horizon ahead with my glass from the royal-yard, when I discovered the French Fleet at anchor in Aboukir Bay. The *Zealous* was so close to us that, had I hailed the deck they must have heard me. I therefore slid down by the backstay and reported what I had seen. We instantly made the signal, but the under-toggle of the upper flag at the main came off, breaking the stop, and the lower flag came down. The compass-signal, however, was clear at the peak. But before we could recover our flag, *Zealous* made the signal for the enemy's fleet. We thus lost the little credit for first signalling the enemy, which, as signal-midshipman, rather affected me.[11]

Rear-Admiral Blanquet, second in command to Admiral Brueys, views the opening scene through French eyes:

The 1st of August, wind N.N.W., light breezes and fine weather. The second division of the fleet sent a party of men on shore, to dig wells. Every ship in the fleet sent twenty-five men to protect the workmen from the continual attacks of the Bedouins and vagabonds of the country.

At two o'clock in the afternoon, *L'Heureux* made signal for twelve sail, W.N.W., which we could easily distinguish from the mast-head to be ships of war. The signal was then made for all the boats, workmen, and guards to repair on board of their respective ships, which was only obeyed by a small number.

At three o'clock, the Admiral not having any doubt but the ships in sight were the enemy, he ordered the hammocks to be stowed for action, and directed *L'Alert* and *Le Railleur* brigs, sloops of war, to reconnoitre the enemy, which we soon perceived were steering for Bequier Bay under a crowd of canvas, but without observing any order of sailing.

At four o'clock, saw over the Fort of Aboukir, two ships [*Alexander* and *Swiftsure*] apparently working to join the squadron: without doubt they had been sent to look into the port at Alexandria. We likewise saw a brig with the ships. In two hours there were fourteen ships of the line in sight, and a brig.

The English fleet was soon off the Island of Bequier. The brig *L'Alert* then began to put the Admiral's orders into execution – viz., to stand toward the enemy until nearly within gunshot, and

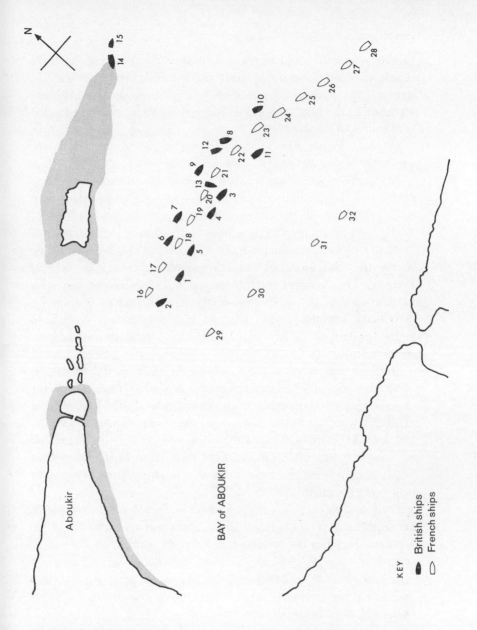

Fig. 5. Plan of the Battle of the Nile based on a plan by Captain Miller, of the *Theseus*. (The *Audacious* (4) was in fact anchored so as to rake the *Conquérant* (17) not as shown by Captain Miller.)

then to manoeuvre and endeavour to draw them toward the outer shoal lying off that island. But the English Admiral, without doubt, had experienced pilots on board, as he did not pay any attention to the brig's track, but allowed her to go away: he hauled well round all the dangers.[4]

In fact, Nelson had before him only a rough drawing of the anchorage, found on board a captured trading vessel.

At four o'clock, a small country-boat dispatched from Alexandria to Rosetta, voluntarily bore down to the English brig, which took possession of her, notwithstanding the repeated efforts of *L'Alert* to prevent it by firing a great many shots at the boat.

At five o'clock, the enemy came to the wind in succession. This manoeuvre convinced us that they intended attacking us that evening. The Admiral got the top gallant yards across, but soon made the signal that he intended engaging the enemy at anchor – convinced, without doubt, that he had not seamen enough to engage under sail; for he wanted at least two-hundred good seamen for each ship.[4]

Blanquet now makes a valid criticism of the French preparation:

After the signal [to engage the enemy at anchor] each ship ought to have sent a stream-cable to the ship astern of her, and to have made a hawser fast to the cable about twenty fathoms in the water, and passed the opposite side to that intended as a spring. This was not generally executed. Orders were then given to let go another bower-anchor, and the broadsides of the ships were brought to bear upon the enemy.[4]

From west to east, in a slight curve, the French Fleet stretched in line a mile and three-quarters. About 160 yards separated the ships. Seaward, they had the protection of a low flat island fortified with a battery of guns and mortars, close to Aboukir Point, the westerly extremity of the bay. Between the island and the point lay reefs and shoals, and for two miles north-east of the island stretched a shoal impassable to all but small ships.

On his journey into exile at St Helena, Napoleon was to ponder Brueys's inferiority as a naval tactician to his opposite number at the Nile. If Brueys had brought his ships closer to each other, cabled, and to the shoals that afforded them natural protection . . .?

Surprise was another element. When the French first sighted the British squadron it was scattered. And to attack, in uncharted waters, just as the sun was going down, seemed unthinkable. But it was the kind of calculated madness for which Nelson was noted. (Later, at Copenhagen, he was again to attack a fleet in a strong anchored position and succeed.)

In such operations the margin between success and failure is wafer thin, but Nelson never lacked nerve or audacity.

Brueys had placed his weaker ships in his protected van, with his stronger ships in the more vulnerable rear. In the centre of the line was his flagship, L'Orient, a giant three-decker, of 120 guns, the most powerful man-of-war in the world.

Nelson threw all the weight of his attack on one point of the French line – and it was the weaker van that received the surprise blow. The French never recovered.

Nelson's Captain, Sir Edward Berry, of the Vanguard, *wrote that at the sight of the French Fleet:*

The utmost joy seemed to animate every breast on board the squadron; and the pleasure which the Admiral himself felt was perhaps more heightened than that of any other man, as he had now a certainty by which he could regulate his future operations.

The Admiral had the highest opinion of, and placed the firmest reliance on, the valour and conduct of every captain in his squadron. It had been his practice during the cruise, whenever the weather and circumstances would permit, to have his captains on board the *Vanguard*, where he would fully develop to them his own ideas of the different and best modes of attack, and such plans as he proposed to execute upon falling in with the enemy, whatever their position or situation might be, by day or by night. With the masterly ideas of their Admiral, therefore, on the subject of naval tactics, every one of the captains of his squadron was most thoroughly acquainted; and upon surveying the situation of the enemy, they could ascertain with precision what were the ideas and intentions of their commander, without the aid of any further instructions; by which means signals became almost unnecessary, much time was saved, and the attention of every captain could almost undistractedly be paid to the conduct of his ship.

The Admiral's mode of attack at anchor, minutely and precisely executed in the action we now come to describe, was planned two months before and the advantage now was that it was familiar to the understanding of every captain in the fleet.

The Admiral made the signal to prepare for battle, and that it was his intention to attack the enemy's van and centre, as they lay at anchor. His idea was first to secure the victory, and then to make the most of it according to future circumstances. A bower cable of each ship was immediately got out abaft, and bent forward. We continued carrying sail, and standing in for the enemy's fleet in a close line of battle. As all the officers of our squadron were totally unacquainted with Aboukir Bay, each ship kept sounding as she stood in.

The enemy appeared to be moored in a strong and compact line of battle, close in with the shore, their line describing an obtuse angle in its form, flanked by numerous gun-boats, four frigates, and a battery of guns and mortars on an island in their van. The situation of the enemy seemed to secure to them the most decided advantages, as they had nothing to attend to but their artillery, in their superior skill in the use of which the French so much prided themselves.

The position of the enemy presented the most formidable obstacles; but the Admiral viewed these with the eye of a seaman determined on attack and it instantly struck his eager and penetrating mind, *that where there was room for an enemy's ship to swing, there was room for one of ours to anchor.* No further signal was necessary than those already made. The Admiral's designs were as fully known to his squadron as was his determination to conquer, or perish in the attempt.

The *Goliath* and *Zealous* had the honour to lead inside . . .[3]

Captain Hood, the Zealous:

As we got abreast of the end of the shaol at the entrance, being within hail of the Admiral and on his lee bow, Sir Horatio asked if I thought we were far enough to the eastward to bear up round the shoal. I told him I was in 11 fathom, that I had no chart of the place, but if he would allow me I would bear up and try with the lead, which I would be attentive to, and lead him as close as I could with safety, it appearing to shoal regularly. He said he would be obliged to me. I then bore away and rounded the shoal, the *Goliath* keeping on my larboard bow, until I found we were advancing too fast for the Admiral. I shortened sail soon after the ship's advancing, and the Admiral only waiting to speak a boat, he made the signal for to proceed on.

The *Goliath* and *Zealous* filled, the *Goliath* ahead and *Zealous* following, and as we approached the van ship of the enemy shortened sail gradually. The Admiral allowing the *Orion* to pass ahead of the *Vanguard*, as well as the *Audacious* and *Theseus*, we had not increased our distance much from those ships. The van ship of the enemy [*Le Guerrier*] being in five fathoms water expected the *Goliath* and *Zealous* to stick on the shoal every moment, and did not imagine we would attempt to pass within her. The van with the mortars, etc., on the island firing regularly at us.

Captain Foley, of course, intended anchoring abreast of the van ship, but his sheet-anchor (the cable being out of the stern port) not dropping the moment he wished it, he missed and brought up abreast of the second ship, having given the van ship his fire. I saw immediately he had failed of his intention, cut away the *Zealous*'s sheet anchor and came to in the exact situation Captain Foley intended to have taken, the van ship of the enemy having his larboard bow toward the *Zealous*. We having received very little damage notwithstanding a fire from the whole van, island, etc., as we came in.

I commenced such a well-directed fire into *Le Guerrier*'s bow within pistol shot a little after six that her fore mast went by the board in about seven minutes, just as the sun was closing the horizon; on which the whole squadron gave three cheers, it happening before the next ship astern of me had fired a shot and only the *Goliath* and *Zealous* engaged. And in ten minutes more her main and mizen masts went; at this time also went the main mast of the second ship, *Le Conquérant*. I could not get *Le Guerrier*'s commander to strike for three hours, though I hailed him twenty times, and seeing he was totally cut up and only firing a stern gun now and then at the *Goliath* and *Audacious*. At last, being tired of firing and killing people in that way, I sent my boat on board her, and the lieutenant was allowed with the jolly-boat to hoist a light and haul it down to show his submission.[15]

Captain Foley's daring in taking Goliath *inside the French line was worthy of his Admiral himself.* Zealous, Theseus, Audacious *and* Orion *followed, despite the navigational risks.*

Midshipman Elliot tells of his Captain's enterprise:

When we were nearly within gunshot, standing as A.D.C. close to Captain Foley, I heard him say to the master that he wished he could get inside the leading ship of the enemy's line, *Le Guerrier*. I immediately looked for the buoy on her anchor, and saw it apparently at the usual distance of a cable's length – i.e. 200 yards – which I reported. They both looked at it, and agreed there was room to pass between the ship and her anchor (the danger was the ship being close to the edge of the shoal), and it was decided to do it. The Master then had orders to go forward and drop the anchor the moment it was a ship's breadth inside the French ship, so that we should not actually swing on board of her. All this was exactly executed.

I also heard Foley say he should not be surprised to find the Frenchman unprepared for action on the inner side; and as we passed her bow I saw he was right. Her lower-deck guns were not run out, and there was lumber, such as bags and boxes, on the upper-deck ports, which I reported with no small pleasure.

We first fired a broadside into the bow. Not a shot could miss at the distance. The *Zealous* did the same, and in less than a quarter of an hour this ship was a perfect wreck, without a mast, or a broadside gun to fire. By this time, having no after-bitts to check the cable by (which came in at the stern port), it kept slowly surging – i.e., slipping – and at last the remaining stoppers broke (our sails had flown·loose by the gear being shot away – we had not time to fold them), and it ran out to the clinch, and placing us a little past the second ship of the French line, so as to engage her and the third ship. We were just in this position when the leading ships of the body of our fleet came in.[11]

Young Elliot had further evidence of the extent to which Nelson had surprised the French:

The French captains were all on board their Admiral's ship, and did not expect us to come in that night. They had sent for their boats to return from the shore where they were procuring water. The senior officer of the van division, seeing us stand on under all sail, got anxious, and sent his own boat to hasten off the boats of his division without waiting to fill with water. She had not got back when we were getting very close, and as his own launch was passing the flagship, half-laden with water, he got into her, but she pulled up slowly against the fresh sea-breeze, and did not reach his ship till we had passed her. I saw him waving his hat, and evidently calling to his ship, when still at a considerable distance. An officer was leaning against his ensign staff listening. At last this officer ran forward to the poop and down to the lower deck. We knew what was coming, and off went their whole broadside, but just too late to hit us, and passed harmlessly between us and *Zealous*, and before he could give a second broadside *Zealous* was past his range. We therefore both got up to our places without injury of any sort, and were able to take up the exact positions we wished, neither ship returning a single shot.

The sun's rim was just touching the horizon as our fire began.

Zealous exactly followed *Goliath*'s example, but the enemy being occupied, she furled her sails, and anchoring a little more to windward, veered into the place just left by the *Goliath*. From this moment the *Guerrier* never fired a shot, except for her stern guns; she had been practically destroyed in five minutes by her two opponents. As the *Goliath* passed her quarter the *Guerrier*'s foremast fell by the deck, and five minutes after the main and mizen fell, and also the main of the *Conquérant*. This was just as the *Orion* was passing inside the *Goliath* and the *Audacious*, coming to anchor on the inner bow of the *Conquérant*.

As the *Theseus* passed the *Goliath* in getting to her station she gave her three tremendous cheers. Returned by the *Goliath*'s crew and an attempt made by the French to copy, but the effort was ridiculous, and caused shouts of laughter in our ships, loud enough to be heard by both sides. The French admitted that the enthusiastic cheers were very disheartening to them.[11]

Captain of the Theseus *was Ralph Miller, who had also commanded the* Captain *and been close to Nelson at St Vincent. In a detailed account of the Battle of the Nile sent to his wife, Captain Miller tells how he had tried to lead into battle:*

When the Admiral hove to, to speak to the *Mutine* about three miles from the enemy, who were making signals and heaving on their springs, I took the opportunity to pass the Admiral to leeward and endeavour to obtain the honour of leading the fleet into battle; but Captain Berry hailed as we passed and gave me the Admiral's order to become his second ahead, in consequence of which I hove-to close ahead of him, and the *Orion* and *Audacious* passed us.

The *Orion*, from her previous situation, described a little wider circle, passed the off side of the *Zealous*, and made a wider sweep in order to come-to with one of her bowers; in doing which she completely knocked up the *Sérieuse* frigate, which lay in her way, having made such a wreck of her that on her driving presently after on a shoal all her masts fell and she filled with water.

I think the *Orion* must have touched the ground from the time between her passing the *Zealous* and her coming-to nearly abreast the inner side of the fifth ship [the *Peuple Souverain*]; for though she passed the *Zealous* before us, we had completely brought up abreast the inner beam of the *Spartiate*, the third ship, and had been in action with her four or five minutes before the *Orion* came-to.[23]

The Culloden, *which had led the line at the battle of St Vincent, fared worse than touching ground. She had cast off a prize, a French wine brig, and was attempting to join the line when she ran aground at the tip of the shoal stretching east from Aboukir Bay. The* Culloden's *log recorded her misfortune:*

Up mainsail, staysail, and spanker, hauled up to clear the *Leander*. Forty minutes past six, struck on a rock and made the

signal No. 43 tabular. *Swiftsure* and *Alexander* astern of us hauled
their wind to clear the reef. The island of Aboukir WSW ¼ W,
distance 2 miles and ¾. The enemy on the island threw several
shells at us, but none reached. Out boats and sounded all round the
ship. Found the most water a cable's length astern and on the
starboard quarter. Put the stream anchor and cable into the
launch and carried it out one cable's length from the ship and
dropped in eleven fathoms water. Sent the launch to the *Mutine*,
who anchored three cables length N by E of us, and took in two
cables and run them to the ship. Took the end in the ward-
room window. Hove taut on both cables and began to start water
in the fore and main holds, and threw the empty casks of the upper
and middle tier overboard.

Found the ship struck very heavy abaft and eased a little
forward. Started the wine in the coal hold and threw a quantity of
bread with provisions of different sorts and the empty wine pipes
overboard as per certificates, and also a great quantity of shot. Also
boats carrying shot, bread, etc., on board the *Mutine* brig.

The swell increasing and the ship striking very heavy, which
knocked her rudder off, which sunk immediately, and from the
violent sending of the ship it carried away the pennants and everything that was fast to it. Found the ship made three feet water per
hour.[20]

The Theseus, *on her way in, had severely punished the unfortunate*
Guerrier:

In running along the enemy's line in the wake of the *Zealous* and
Goliath [wrote Captain Miller], I observed their shot sweep just
over us, and knowing well that at such a moment Frenchmen
would not have coolness enough to change their elevation, I closed
them suddenly, and running under the arch of their shot reserved
my fire, every gun being loaded with two and some with three
round shot, until I had the *Guerrier*'s masts in a line, and her
jib-boom about six feet clear of our rigging. We then opened with
such effect that a second breath could not be drawn before her
main and mizen mast were also gone; this was precisely at sunset,
or forty-four minutes past six; then, passing between her and the

Zealous, and as close as possible round the off side of the *Goliath*, we anchored exactly in line with her, and abreast the *Spartiate*. The *Audacious* having passed between the *Guerrier* and the *Conquérant*, came-to with her bower close upon the inner bow of the latter. We had not been many minutes in action with the *Spartiate* when we observed *Vanguard* place herself so directly opposite to us on the outside of her that I desisted firing on her, and directed every gun before the main mast on the *Aquilon*, and all abaft it on the *Conquérant*, and giving up my proper bird to the Admiral.

The *Minotaur*, following the Admiral, placed herself on the outer side of the fourth ship, the *Aquilon*, and the *Defence* on the fifth, the *Peuple Souverain*.

The *Bellerophon* dropped her stern anchor well on the outer bow of *L'Orient*, the seventh ship, but it not bringing her up she became singly opposed to the fire of that enormous ship before her own broadside completely bore, and then sustained the greater part of her loss. She then drifted along the French line and came to anchor about six miles eastward of us, where we discovered her next morning, without a mast standing, with her ensign on the stump of the main mast. Captain Darby was wounded at the beginning, and poor Daniel, 1st Lieutenant, as well as the 2nd and 4th, killed.

The *Majestic*, whether owing to the thickness of the smoke at the shutting in of the evening or that her stern cable did not bring her up in time, ran her jib-boom into the main rigging of *L'Heureux*, ninth ship, and remained a long time in that unfortunate position suffering greatly. Poor Captain Wescott was almost the first that fell, being killed by a musket-ball in the neck. She got disentangled, and brought her broadside to bear on the starboard bow of the *Mercure*, tenth ship, on whom she took a severe revenge; having laid that bow almost open, she also had only a foremast standing at daylight.

My worthy friends, Captains Hallowell [*Swiftsure*] and Ball [*Alexander*] got among us a few minutes after eight o'clock, the *Swiftsure* coming-to, with her stern anchor upon the outer quarter of the *Franklin* (sixth ship) and bow of *L'Orient*, so as to fire into both, and the *Alexander* bringing up with her stern anchor close upon the inner quarter of *L'Orient*.

When the five headmost ships of the enemy were completely subdued, which might have been about nine or half-past, the *Leander* came-to with her stern anchor upon the inner bow of the *Franklin*, being thus late by proffering assistance to the *Culloden*.[23]

By the judicious disposition of the British squadron [recalled Midshipman Lee of the *Swiftsure*] the half of the French fleet were exposed to the fire of the whole of the British anchored on either side of them; while at the same time the windward portion of them being first attacked, those to leeward could consequently render the others no assistance during the battle; with the exception of the *Tonnant*, which being the weathermost of the French unengaged ships, by hauling her broadside in a raking position across the British line, caused severe loss to the *Majestic* and *Swiftsure*. The *Majestic* never quitted her station, although she had her captain and two-hundred of her crew killed and wounded in a very short space of time.[18]

Midshipman John Theophilus Lee was on the day of the battle not yet 11 years old. He remembered the confusion that the darkness often caused:

Each British ship had been directed to hoist four lanthorns on a horizontal pole at the mizen peak, as a distinguishing mark, but these being often shot away, and the night rendered still more dark by the cannon smoke, consequently the *Swiftsure* and *Alexander*, which came late into action, were greatly puzzled where to take their stations; the former even being on the point of firing into the *Bellerophon*, which dismasted and without colours or distinguishing lanthorns was found drifting out of the battle. Her position in the line was promptly taken by *Swiftsure*, but more upon *L'-Orient*'s bow, whereby she was less exposed to the latter's powerful battery.[18]

Young Lee had gazed in awe upon the French flagship on his first sight of the enemy fleet in Aboukir Bay:

... the tremendous four-decked *L'Orient* lying in the centre, with an immense French admiral's flag flying at the main; this huge ship towered like a castle over all the others around her, although some of them were 84's of the first class. All the small 74's, of which the English fleet were principally composed, appeared like frigates alongside of them . . . .[18]

For Midshipman Lee the end of L'Orient *was to be an even more awe-inspiring sight, vividly recalled forty years later:*

The cannonading between the rear ships of the two fleets was much more destructive than that between those of the van; the disappearance of daylight only seeming to increase the fury of the contest; the incessant flashings of the numerous guns, discharged at nearly the same instant, being so vivid at times as to enable each party to distinguish clearly, not only the colours of the respective combatants, but the disastrous results of the battle upon them.

Being aid-de-camp to Captain Hallowell, I was sent by him during the hottest period of the fight to bring a few bottles of ginger beer from the cabin locker round the mizen mast, for the refreshment of himself and other officers actively engaged on the quarter-deck, and of which also I partook, when Captain Hallowell after remarking to me that the ship the *Swiftsure* was opposed to fired extremely well turned away from the gang-way where we had both hitherto stood during the whole of the action, but had not long left it before a heavy shot shivered the place to pieces, scattering the splinters for a considerable distance round.

Shortly after Captain Hallowell, observing an appearance of fire in the mizen chains of *L'Orient*, ordered me to run below and desire Lieutenants Waters, the Hon. F. Aylmer, Davis, and Mudge to point every gun that would bear upon this spot, to which also the musketry of the marines stationed upon the poop, under Captain Allen, was directed, with a view of preventing the enemy from extinguishing the conflagration; and with such effective results that all their efforts to subdue it were rendered unavailing, by the slaughter which the concentrated fire of the *Swiftsure* produced. The conflagration soon began to rage with dreadful fury; but the Frenchmen, nothing daunted, still gloriously maintained the honour of their favourite flag.

The brave Brueys, the French commander-in-chief, having lost both his legs, was seated with tourniquets on the stumps, in an armchair facing his enemy, and giving directions for extinguishing the fire, when a cannonball from the western side of the *Swiftsure* put a period to his gallant life, by nearly cutting him in two. The son of Casabianca, the captain of the fleet, had lost a leg and was below with the surgeon; but the father could not be prevailed on to quit the ship even to save his own life, preferring to die beside the son, rather than leave him wounded, and a prey to the flames, thus placing parental affection in a most trying and awful situation, as if to show the extremities to which it may be carried.[18]

Blanquet says father and 10-year-old son were last seen in the sea, clinging to L'Orient's *wrecked mast. Whatever their eventual fate, the incident was the origin of a highly popular poem* – The Boy Stood on the Burning Deck, *by Mrs Hemans.*

Midshipman Lee continues:

The fire soon ran up the rigging and along the yards and decks, but the honour of the French flag was nobly sustained; for although the flames obliged the people to desert their guns on the gang-ways and maindeck, the middle and lower decks still struggled for victory by the keeping up of a most heavy and destructive cannonade.

It was only after the fire had so beautifully, but awfully illumined the whole of both lines, that the *Swiftsure* was discovered by the rest of the fleet to have been engaging this enormous four-decked ship; the men from which began to jump overboard from the head and quarter; and many must have been dashed to pieces in the water by the showers of flying shot.

The *Swiftsure* was so near the burning *L'Orient* that the pitch ran out of her seams in streamlets down the side; the momentarily expected explosion of the immense ship beside her causing great alarm, lest she should be involved in the same awful catastrophe. Several of the seamen wished the cable to be slipped, but the brave and determined Hallowell saw, with the eye of judgment, that her present station was the best calculated to secure her from danger, as the explosion would naturally throw all up into the air in the shape of an arch, and the *Swiftsure* being, as may be supposed, near the centre thereof, consequently the greater part of the fragments would naturally be projected over and beyond her. Two sentinels were therefore placed by the cable round the mizen mast, with directions to shoot anyone who might attempt to cut it; while the ports were ordered to be lowered, the magazines and hatchways closed, and every man to go under cover, provided with wet swabs and buckets of water, in order to extinguish any burning fragments that might come on board during the explosion.

At this moment the scene was awfully grand: each fleet as if by consent had ceased from firing, the wind had fallen to a calm from the heavy discharging of artillery, and all seemed to await in suspense the eventful moment, with a feeling of anxiety indescribable, when so many brave men were to be launched into eternity.

The flames had now reached below the lower decks of the enemy's ship; but still the proud silk flag of her fallen chief seemed to float untouched amidst them. Nelson, forgetful of his own wounds, hearing from his captain of the expected fate of his rival Admiral, came on deck and ordered every boat to be dispatched to save the crew of the devoted vessel – the cold, clear, placid light of the moon formed a striking contrast with that of the burning ship, and enabled the lines of the hostile fleets to be, for the first time, clearly distinguished – so gratifying to the one and so mortifying to the other.

Every moment the dreadful explosion was expected – the least noise could now be heard, where the din of war before raged with such incontrollable violence – till at last an awful and terrific glare of light blinding the very sight showed *L'Orient* blowing up, with an astounding crash, paralyzing all around her, by which near a thousand brave spirits were hastened into eternity.

A large ignited beam fell into the foretop of the *Swiftsure* and set it on fire, but the flames were soon extinguished; other and heavier pieces bounding against the sides or into the chains, and some even upon the decks and booms, but all being speedily prevented from doing mischief by the active measures employed; the greater portion, as anticipated, passing clear over the mast heads and falling in the sea a considerable way beyond the tremendous explosion; however it shook the ship more than the whole battle. It was like an earthquake, the air rushing along the decks and below with inconceivable violence, and creating a tremulous motion in the ship, which existed for some minutes, and was awfully grand.[18]

A chaplain, the Rev. Cooper Willyams, had also had a close view from the Swiftsure *of the blazing* L'Orient, *and witnessed the dreadful predicament of her crew:*

The men of the *Swiftsure* did all they could to rescue those of the crew who had committed themselves to the waves before the explosion, ropes, spars, gratings, everything buoyant being flung to the men and every endeavour made to save life.

Several of the officers and men, seeing the impracticability of extinguishing the fire, which had now extended itself along the upper-decks and was flaming up the masts, jumped overboard, some supporting themselves on spars and pieces of wreck, others swimming with all their might to escape the dreaded catastrophe. Shot flying in all directions dashed many of them to pieces; others were picked up by boats of the fleet, or dragged into the lower ports of the nearest ships. The British sailors humanely stretched forth their hands to save a fallen enemy, though the battle at that moment raged with uncontrollable fury. The *Swiftsure*, that was anchored within half-pistol shot of the larboard bow of *L'Orient*, saved the lives of the Commissary, First-Lieutenant, and ten men, who were drawn out of the water into the lower-deck ports during the hottest part of the action.[40]

First-Lieutenant Berthelot had been naked in the sea, when the thought struck him that unless he could be identified as an officer he had a poor chance of rescue. He accordingly swam back to L'Orient, *now ablaze from stem to stern, found, with difficulty, his discarded clothes on the quarter-deck, and selected one item. Shortly afterwards he appeared before Captain Hallowell on the* Swiftsure, *wearing only a cocked-hat:*

'*Who the deuce are you, sir?*'

'*Je suis de* L'Orient, *monsieur.*'

The surprise attack of the British ships from both sides had crushed all resistance from the French van, as Miller relates:

The *Guerrier* and *Conquérant* made a very inefficient resistance, the latter being soon stripped of her main and mizen masts. They continued for a considerable time to fire, every now and then, a gun or two, and about eight o'clock, I think, were totally silent.

The *Spartiate* resisted much longer, and with serious effect, as the *Vanguard*'s killed and wounded announces, who received her principal fire; her larboard guns were fired upon us in the beginning with great quickness, but after the Admiral anchored on his starboard side, it was slow and irregular, and before or about nine o'clock she was silenced, and had also lost her main and mizen masts.

The *Aquilon* was silenced a little earlier, with the loss of all her masts, having the whole fire of the *Minotaur* on her starboard side, and for some time near half ours on her larboard bow.

Le Peuple Souverain was, about the same time, entirely dismasted and silenced and drifting between the *Franklin* and *Orion*, when the *Leander* came into the battle and took her place immediately on the *Franklin*'s larboard bow, the *Swiftsure* having been long on her starboard quarter, and *Defence*, after *Le Peuple Souverain* drifted away, firing upon her starboard bow.[23]

The situation was hopeless for the French. Their van had been conquered; their Commander-in-Chief, Admiral Brueys, was dead, and their new commander, Rear-Admiral Blanquet, on Le Franklin, *injured; their most powerful ship, and largest man-of-war in the world, had been destroyed in an explosion heard and witnessed by people standing on eminences at Rosetta, ten miles away.*

Immediately after the explosion, Chaplin Willyams observed that:

An awful silence reigned for several minutes, as if the contending squadrons, struck with horror at the dreadful event, which in an instant had hurled so many brave men into the air, had forgotten their hostile rage in pity for the sufferers.[40]

Not everyone. Ralph Miller shared Nelson's hatred of the French:

L'Orient, in a blaze, displaying a most grand and awful spectacle,

1. Head of the Nelson effigy in Westminster Abbey, modelled by
Catherine Andras.

2. Earl St Vincent, who early recognized Nelson's naval genius.
From an engraving by Ridley, after Abbott.

3. (*below*) The Battle of Cape St Vincent.
From an engraving by J. Bailey, after T. Whitcombe.

4. (*right*) Nelson boarding the *San Nicolas*.
After Frank Baden-Powell.

5. Nelson receives
   the Spanish
   Admiral's sword.
   From an engraving
   by R. Goldring,
   after R. Westall.

6. Sir Horatio
   Nelson, when
   wounded at
   Tenerife on the
   night of 24 July
   1797.
   From an engraving
   by J. Neagle, after
   R. Westall.

7. Cuthbert, Lord
   Collingwood ('old
   Cuddy').
   From an engraving
   by W. Holl.

8. Emma Hamilton,
   1791.
   From a drawing
   by Sir Thomas
   Lawrence.

9. *The Battle of the Nile, at 10 o'clock at night.*
   Painted and engraved by R. Dodd.

10. *L'Orient* blows up.
    From an engraving by J. Bailey, after T. Whitcombe.

11. Nelson on the quarter-deck of the *Vanguard*.
From a painting by Daniel Orme.

12. The Battle of Copenhagen.
From an engraving by T. Sutherland, after T. Whitcombe.

13. The Defeat of the Danish Fleet and Batteries off Copenhagen. From an engraving by P. W. Tomkins, after I. T. Serres.

14. Fairburn's plan of victory before Copenhagen.

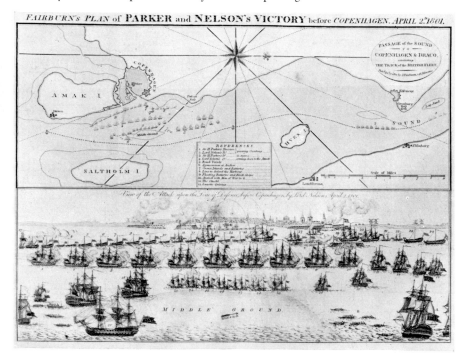

15. Nelson leaving Portsmouth for the last time.
From a painting in the Royal Exchange by Andrew C. Gow.

Memo   Victory off Cadiz 9 Oct[r]
                                                    1805

Thinking it almost impossible to bring
a fleet of forty Sail of the Line into a
Line of Battle in variable winds thick
weather and other circumstances which
must occur, without such a loss of
time that the opportunity would
probably be lost of bringing the
Enemy to Battle in such a manner
as to make the business decisive.—
    I have therefore made up my mind to
keep the fleet in that position of
Sailing (with the exception of the first
and second in command) that the order
of Sailing is to be the order of Battle, the
placing the fleet in two Lines of Sixteen
Ships each with an advanced Squadron

16. Nelson's memo to his captains before Trafalgar.

17. Trafalgar: broaching the enemy's line.
From an engraving by T. Sutherland, after T. Whitcombe.
18. The Battle of Trafalgar at its height.
From an engraving by T. Sutherland, after T. Whitcombe.

19. Nelson on the quarter-deck of the *Victory*.
    From a colour print by Overend.

20. Nelson falls.
    From an engraving by J. Heath, after B. West.

21. Death of Nelson.
From an engraving by William Bromley, after A. W. Davis.

22. Key to A. W. Davis's painting of the death of Nelson.

H.M.S. IMPLACABLE
74 GUNS
Formerly French Duguay Trouin
built at Rochefort. 1800
fought at Trafalgar
captured 1805
towed to Sea and sunk 1950

23. (*left*) Figurehead of Rear-Admiral Dumanoir's flagship, the *Duguay-Trouin*, captured shortly after Trafalgar and renamed *Implacable*.

24. (*above*) Lord Nelson's funeral procession by water, from Greenwich Hospital to Whitehall, 8 January 1806.
From an engraving by J. Clarke and H. Marke, after Turner.

25. (*below*) The shallop which carried Nelson's body by water.

26. The funeral procession reaches St Paul's Cathedral.
From an engraving by J. Godby, after W. M. Craig.

such as formerly would have drawn tears down the victor's cheeks, but now pity was stifled as it rose by the remembrance of the numerous and horrid atrocities their unprincipled and bloodthirsty nation had and were committing; and when she blew up, about eleven o'clock, though I endeavoured to stop the momentary cheer of the ship's company, my heart scarce felt a single pang for their fate. Indeed, all its anxiety was in a moment called forth to a degree of terror for her, at seeing the *Alexander* on fire in several places; and a boat that was taking in a hawser, in order to warp the *Orion* further from *L'Orient*, I filled with fire-buckets and sent instantly to her, and was putting the engine in another just returned from sounding, when I had the unspeakable happiness of seeing her get before the wind and extinguish the flames.[23]

Nelson considered the battle to have been won even before L'Orient *blew up a few hours after nightfall on 1st August. About 8.00 p.m. he had been standing with Berry on the quarter-deck of the* Vanguard, *when he was struck on the head by a piece of the scrapshot the French were using to destroy the British sails – his brow was ripped to the bone just above the good eye, a flap of flesh, followed by a rush of blood, blinding him. He collapsed in Berry's arms, murmuring: 'I am killed. Remember me to my wife.'*

The Vanguard, *caught in cross-fire from* L'Aquilon *and* Le Spartiate, *might have been forced to haul out of line had not the* Minotaur *under Captain Thomas Louis come to his Admiral's relief.*

By 8.30 p.m. Le Spartiate *had ceased to fire. Berry sent First-Lieutenant Galwey and a party of marines to board her; the former returned with the French commander's sword for delivery to Nelson. His wound was not as serious as it looked, and, his head bandaged, he had been able to appear for a few minutes on deck to gaze on the blazing* L'Orient *and to appreciate that victory was his. It must have been a satisfying sight, but Captin Berry reported that:*

The first consideration that struck his mind was concern for the danger of so many lives, to save as many as possible. A boat, the only one that could swim, was instantly dispatched from the

Vanguard, and other ships that were in a condition to do so immediately followed the example; by which means the lives of about seventy Frenchmen were saved.[3]

Admiral Blanquet had, like Nelson, been wounded in the head and carried below. In his account of the battle he gave details of Le Franklin's *ordeal:*

At half-past nine, Citizen Gillet, Capitaine de Pavillon of *Le Franklin* was very severely wounded, and carried off the deck. At three-quarters past nine, the arms-chest, filled with musket-cartridges, blew up and set fire to several places on the poop and quarter-deck, but was fortunately extinguished. The situation, however, was still very desperate; surrounded by enemies and only eighty fathoms to windward of *L'Orient* (entirely on fire), there could not be any other expectation than falling a prey either to the enemy or the flames. At ten o'clock the main and mizen masts fell, and all the guns on the main deck were dismounted.

The explosion of *L'Orient* was dreadful, and spread the fire all round to a considerable distance. *Le Franklin*'s decks were with red-hot pincers, pieces of timber, and rope, on fire. She was on fire the fourth time, but luckily got it under.

Immediately after the tremendous explosion the action ceased everywhere, and was succeeded by the most profound silence. The sky was obscured by thick clouds of black smoke, which seemed to threaten the destruction of the two fleets. It was a quarter of an hour before the ships' crews recovered from the kind of stupor they were thrown into.[4]

It was Le Franklin *that broke the awe-struck silence.*

Towards eleven o'clock [continued Blanquet], *Le Franklin*, anxious to preserve the trust confided to her, recommenced the action with a few of her lower-deck guns; all the rest were dismounted, two-thirds of her ship's company being killed or wounded, and those who remained much fatigued. She was surrounded by enemy ships, some of which were within pistol-shot, and who mowed down the men every broadside. At half-past eleven o'clock, having only three lower-deck guns that could defend the honour of the flag, it became necessary to put an end to so disproportioned a struggle; and Citizen Martinet ordered the colours to be struck.[4]

John Theophilus Lee:

All the boats of the *Swiftsure* being cut to pieces, Captain Peyton, *Defence*, was requested to board and take possession of *Le Franklin.* The *Swiftsure, Alexander,* and *Majestic,* being the only British ships now engaged with that part of the French fleet to leeward, who had not borne the brunt of the action; those to windward having previously struck to the *Goliath, Zealous, Orion, Vanguard, Minotaur,* and *Audacious. Le Tonnant* had been roughly handled by *Majestic* and had lost all her masts; while *L'Heureux, Le Mercure,* and *Le Timoléon,* of 74 guns each, were on shore to leeward near the mouth of the Nile. *Le Guillaume Tell,* of 84 guns, and *Le Généreux,* of 78 guns, with the *Justice* and *Diane* frigates alone appeared capable of moving. At three o'clock, a.m., as daylight began to dawn, both fleets seemed to be exhausted, and the firing ceased about four, for a short period on both sides.[18]

The exhaustion experienced by the crew of Miller's Theseus *was probably general:*

My people were so extremely jaded that as soon as they had hove our sheet anchor up they dropped under the capstan-bars, and were asleep in a moment in every sort of posture, having been then working at their fullest exertion, or fighting, for near twelve hours.[23]

For that gritty mariner, John Nicol, on the active Goliath, *it had been 'the busiest night in my life'. In his memoir of a hard life at sea, he further commented:*

I saw as little of this action as I did of the one on February 14th off Cape St Vincent.[30]

But Nicol's account of the Nile brings home to us the bravery, pathos, and horror below deck in a fierce and prolonged sea-battle, for the men and (surprisingly) women there:

My station was in the powder magazine with the gunner. As we entered the bay, we stripped to our trousers, opened our ports, cleared, and every ship we passed gave them a broadside and three cheers. Any information we got was from the boys and women who carried the powder. The women behaved as well as the men, and got a present for their bravery from the Grand Signior.

When the French Admiral's ship blew up, the *Goliath* got such a shake we thought the after-part of her had blown up until the boys told us what it was. They brought us every now and then the cheering news of another French ship having struck, and we answered the cheers on deck with heart-felt joy.

In the heat of the action, a shot came right into the magazine, but did no harm, as the carpenters plugged it up and stopped the water that was rushing in.

I was much indebted to the gunner's wife, who gave her husband and me a drink of wine every now and then, which lessened our fatigue much. There were some women wounded, and one woman belonging to Leith died of her wounds, and was buried on a small island in the bay. One woman bore a son in the heat of the action; she belonged to Edinburgh.

When we ceased firing, I went on deck to view the state of the fleets, and an awful sight it was. The whole bay was covered with dead bodies, mangled, wounded and scorched, not a bit of clothes on them except their trousers.

There were a number of French, belonging to the French Admiral's ship, *L'Orient*, who had swam to the *Goliath*, and were cowering under her forecastle. Poor fellows, they were brought on board, and Captain Foley ordered them down to the steward's room to get provisions and clothing. One thing I observed in these Frenchmen quite different from anything I had ever before observed. In the American war, when we took a French ship, the *Duke de Chartres*, the prisoners were as merry as if they had taken us, only saying, 'Fortune de guerre' – you take me today, I take you tomorrow. Those we now had on board were thankful for our kindness, but were sullen and as downcast as if each had lost a ship of his own.

The only incidents I heard of are two. One lad who was stationed by a salt-box, on which he sat to give out cartridges and keep the lid close – it is a trying birth – when asked for a cartridge, he gave none, yet he sat upright; he eyes were open. One of the men gave him a push; he fell all his length on the deck. There was not a blemish on his body, yet he was quite dead, and was thrown overboard.

The other, a lad who had the match in his hand to fire his gun. In the act of applying it a shot took off his arm; it hung by a small piece of skin. The match fell to the deck. He looked to his arm, and seeing what had happened, seized the match in his left hand and fired the gun before he went off to the cock-pit to have it dressed.

They were in our mess, or I might never have heard of it. Two of the mess were killed, and I knew not of it until the day after.[30]

That the Theseus *was one of the least damaged British ships reveals the ferocity of the battle:*

We were now thus situated in the *Theseus* [wrote Miller]: our mizen mast so badly wounded that it could bear no sail; our fore and main yard so badly wounded that I almost expected them to come down about our ears, without sail; the fore-topmast and bowsprit wounded; the fore and main sail cut to pieces, and most of the other sails much torn; nine of our main, and several fore and mizen shrouds, and much of our other standing and running rigging shot away; eight guns disabled, either from the deck being ploughed up under themselves, or carriages struck by shot, or the axle-trees breaking from the heat of the fire; and four of them lower deckers. In men we were fortunate beyond anything I ever saw or heard of; for though near eighty large shot struck our hull, and some of them through both sides, we had only six men killed and thirty-one wounded. Providence, in its goodness, seemed willing to make up to us for our heavy loss at Santa Cruz.[23]

In spite of the doubtful condition of his ship, Captain Miller was eager for what amounted to mopping up operations after sunrise on 2nd August. He describes the concluding stage of a battle already devastatingly won:

Precisely at sunrise I opened fire on *Le Guillaume Tell* and *Le Généreux*, as the *Alexander* and *Majestic* did immediately after; this was directly returned, principally by *Le Guillaume Tell* and *Le Tonnant*. After a little time, perceiving they all increased their distance, we veered to two cables on each anchor, and soon after the *Leander* came down, and having anchored without the *Alexander*, commenced a very distant fire. These four ships, having at length by imperceptible degrees got almost to the utmost range of shot, we turned our whole fire upon the two line-of-battle ships that were on our quarter, and whom we had now long known to be on shore.

In a short time we compelled *L'Heureux*, 74, to strike her colours, and I sent Lieutenant Brodie to take possession of her, and from her to hail the other ship to strike immediately, or she would else soon be involved in so much smoke and fire that we, not being able to see her colours come down, might, unintentionally, destroy all on board her. Just as the boat got there, the *Goliath* anchored on our outer quarter and began to fire, but desisted on my hailing her; and presently after, *Le Mercure*, 74, hauled her colours down; also as *L'Artémise*, 36, after firing her guns shotted, had done just before.

I sent Lieutenant Hawkins to take possession of *Le Mercure*, and Lieutenant Hoste of *L'Artémise*. The former, on a lieutenant of the *Alexander* afterwards coming, delivered her into his charge, and returned on board; and when the latter got within about a cable's length of *L'Artémise*, perceiving she was set on fire by a train, and that her people had abandoned her on the opposite side, he also returned on board. After burning about half an hour, she blew up. This dishonourable action was not out of character for a modern Frenchman.

The enemy were anchored again at the long range of shot, and many large boats from the shore were passing to and fro among them. The frigate, *La Justice*, was playing about under sail, and at length stood out of the bay, as if to make her escape. *Zealous* was standing down towards us, but stood out again as the Admiral made her signal to chase the frigate, who stood back into the bay, *Zealous* remaining outside.

Hearing it was the enemy's intention to take their men out of their line-of-battle ships and set them on fire – for, we supposed them on shore, ourselves in $4\frac{1}{2}$ fathoms – I caused a cool and steady fire to be opened on them from our lower decks only. This soon drove the boats entirely away from all their ships, and doubtless hulled them frequently, particularly *Le Timoléon*.

The boats having abandoned them, *Le Guillaume Tell*, *Le Généreux*, *Le Timoléon*, with the frigates *La Justice* and *La Diane*, got under way, and stood out in the bay in line of battle. *Le Timoléon*, being under our fire all the time, cast in shore, and, after appearing to make another attempt to wear, stood directly for the shore, and, as she struck, her foremast went over the bows. *Le Tonnant*, being dismasted, remained where she was.

The Admiral made the *Zealous*, *Goliath*, *Audacious*, and *Leander* signals to chase the others. *Zealous* very gallantly pushed at them alone, and exchanged broadsides as she past close on the different tacks; but they had so much start of the other ships, and now of the *Zealous*, who had suffered much in her rigging, and knowing also they were remarkably fast sailers, the Admiral made the general signal of recall, and these four ships were soon out of sight.[23]

In the evening Miller visited Nelson:

... who I before knew was wounded. I found him in his cot, weak but in good spirits, and, as I believed every Captain did, received his warmest thanks, which I could return from my heart, for the promptness and gallantry of the attack. I found him naturally anxious to secure *Le Tonnant* and *Le Timoléon*, and *Leander* was ordered to go down for that purpose in the morning. I told him if there was any difficulty I would also go down in the morning, notwithstanding the state of the ship.[23]

Le Tonnant *offered a last brief defiance:*

Seeing *Leander* get under weigh we hove up our best bower [continued Miller], sent our prisoners and their baggage, which lumbered our guns, on board *Goliath*, and got a slip buoy on the end of the sheet cable. *Swiftsure*'s boat returning from having been with a flag of truce to summons *Le Tonnant*, informed us the answer of the Captain was that he had 1600 men on board, and unless the Admiral would give him a ship to convey them to Toulon, he would fight to the last man – a true French gasconade. We immediately slipped the sheet cable, and hoisted our topsails, and seeing the Admiral make *Leander's* signal to engage the enemy, which must have been the moment of his receiving this French reply, we hove up our best bower and ran down directly for *Le Tonnant*, with the Master sounding in a boat ahead. As we cast so as to open the view of our broadsides to her, she hoisted truce colours. Just after we came to, in $25\frac{1}{2}$ feet water, she allowed *Leander's* boat to come on board, and was soon after under English colours.

Le Timoléon, being abandoned by her crew, was set on fire with her colours flying, and soon blew up.

There being no longer an enemy to contend with, we beat the retreat and solemnly returned thanks to Almighty God through whose mercy we had been instrumental in obtaining so great and glorious a victory to His Majesty's arms.[23]

Shortly after appearing, bandaged, on deck to observe the spectacle of the blazing L'Orient, Nelson had summoned his secretary to take down a despatch to Earl St Vincent, but at the sight of the seemingly blinded Admiral the secretary was so overcome that he could not write. Nelson impatiently pushed aside the bandage and himself began the first draft of the despatch. The final version is dated 3rd August:

My Lord,

Almighty God has blessed His Majesty's arms in the late battle, by a great victory over the fleet of the enemy, who I attacked at sunset on the 1st August, off the mouth of the Nile. The enemy were moored in a strong line of battle for defending the entrance of the Bay of Shoals flanked by numerous gun-boats, four frigates, and a battery of guns and mortars on an island in their van: but nothing could withstand the squadron your Lordship did me the honour to place under my command. Their high state of discipline is well known to you, and with the judgement of the captains, together with their valour, and that of the officers and men of every description, it was absolutely irresistible. Could anything from my pen add to the character of the captains, I would write it with pleasure, but that is impossible.

I have to regret the loss of Captain Westcott of the *Majestic*, who was killed early in the action: but the ship was continued to .be so well fought by her first lieutenant, Mr. Cuthbert, that I have given him an order to command her till your Lordship's pleasure is known.

The ships of the enemy, all but their two rear ships, are nearly dismasted: and those two, with two frigates, I am sorry to say, made their escape; nor was it, I assure you, in my power to prevent them. Captain Hood most handsomely endeavoured to do it, but I had no ship in a condition to support the *Zealous*, and I was obliged to call her in.

The support and assistance I have received from Captain Berry cannot be sufficiently expressed. I was wounded in the head, and obliged to be carried off the deck: but the service suffered no loss by that event: Captain Berry was fully equal to the important service then going on, and to him I must beg leave to refer you for any information relative to this victory. He will present you with the Flag of the Second in Command, that of the Commander-in-Chief being burnt in *L'Orient* . . .

I have the honour to be, my Lord, your Lordship's most obedient servant,

Horatio Nelson.[27]

Nelson included with his despatch lists of ships and casualties. He estimated the French killed or missing as 5,235. Three French captains had been killed and 7 wounded. He kept 200 prisoners to serve the fleet, and sent 3,105 ashore. The British casualties were 218 killed and 677 wounded. The French casualties were a little less: Nelson's figures were based on their ships' full complement and did not allow for the failure of working parties to return from the mainland.

It was two months and a day before London received Nelson's account of his victory.

Berry was ordered to carry the despatch home in Leander. *In case of misfortune, duplicates were to be taken in* Mutine *to Naples (now under command of Lieutenant Capel, Captain Hardy having taken over from Berry on the* Vanguard). *The precaution was justified.* Leander *sailed on 6th August and had the misfortune to*

run into the escaping Le Généreux *on the 18th. The French ship had
74 guns to* Leander's *50, and by then 900 men to her opponent's 300.
Nevertheless,* Leander *fought one of the most courageous defences in
British naval history, here described by one of her main-deck gunners,
Tim Stewart, when a pensioner at Greenwich Hospital:*

After the Nile action, our ship being in the best state, she was
ordered to carry the account of the action to the Admiral of the
station, and Captain Berry, Lord Nelson's Flag-Captain, was sent
on board with the despatches, for a passage. Just eighteen days
after the action, at day-break in the morning, our ship was becalmed under the island of Candia, when we saw a large ship
standing towards us with a light breeze. We soon made her out to
be one of the Nile ships, because of the white patches over the
shot-holes about her bows, and, accordingly, cleared for action.
You see, we couldn't get away if we had tried, because the ship
was land-locked; so the Captain ordered the ship to be kept as
she was going. We didn't take long to clear for action.

We piped to breakfast at one bell in the morning watch. I
suppose our captain thought the French wouldn't give us a belly-
full; be that as it may, we went to breakfast upon cold water and
biscuit, and many a poor fellow never had another. We had about
fifteen hands wounded, lying in their hammocks, when we
commenced the action, who got hurt at the Nile. Poor fellows! We
had lost nearly a hundred men, killed and wounded, before we
struck. Well, as soon as we had done breakfast – not long, you may
be sure, when our enemy was in sight – the drum beat to quarters.

I was doing quartermaster's duty at that time, though rather a
young hand, and 'twas my watch on deck when we first made her
out. When they beat to quarters after breakfast, I gave up the
wheel to the Captain's coxswain and went to my quarters on the
main-deck. About one bell in the forenoon watch, up came the
Frenchman, blazing away, right and left, long before she was in
gun-shot, and wasting the powder and shot which we wanted.

When she came pretty close, the word was passed to lie down at
our quarters, as usual, to receive a broadside; and she began to hit
us, but hurt no one. At last all as quiet below as house-breakers,

we had the word of command given us – 'Fire!' The Frenchman was close alongside, and we gave him as smart a broadside as our little guns, double-shotted, could throw. He then run us aboard by the forechains, and tried to board, but they got off with the worst of it. Our division of boarders was called up from below, to lend a hand to keep them off, and one fellow struck the point of a boarding-pike in my cheek.

Well, our mizen mast was shot away, and a breeze coming off the land, the French ship got ahead of us, and we managed to get a chance of raking her. We poured every shot of our broadside into her cabin windows, and sent many a Johnny-Crappo to the bar of the other world. But it soon came to their turn, and they fired their whole broadside into us, within pistol shot. It shook us from stem to stern, and many a poor fellow lost the number of his mess.

We fought six hours; just think of that. Why, if she had handled her guns in a seamanlike manner, she ought to have sunk us in little more than six minutes. We had to cut through the main top-sail, lying over our larboard side, to make room for the muzzles of the guns, for our ship was quite a wreck – not a stick standing – but still the brave hearts wouldn't give in. Fore and aft there was no murmur heard, every man was ready to stick by the craft till she sunk; and once, when *Le Généreux* sheered off to repair some damages, we gave him three cheers, and turned-to, making cart-ridges, and refitting all we could to give him chase. We fired everything at him we could get hold of – crow-bars, nails, and all sorts. I saw one of the crow-bars sticking through her deck afterwards; and they never had a harder day's work in their lives than when they took the little *Leander*. We killed nearly three hundred of them before we surrendered. But we lost two lieuten-ants, the master, the boatswain, and a third part of the crew; and the great lubberly hulk had taken up his birth under our stern, to give us another broadside, when our brave captain, thinking we had fought long enough, for it was now past five bells in the afternoon watch, ordered our colours to be hauled down; and the old English Ensign, all in strips, was struck . . . .[37]

At the same time, Nelson's despatches and letters from the British squadron were sent to the bottom of the sea in three sacks loaded with shot.

. . . As soon as the Frenchmen saw we had struck, one of their midshipmen and two or three men swam on board of us (for neither had a boat that could swim). They were stark naked, and they dived down below at once, and rigged themselves in any clothes they could get hold of. Not one of us offered the least resistance. At last the Frenchmen managed to mend one of their boats with tarpaulins, so as to get us aboard their ship. We had not many traps left us to take away, for lots of the Frenchmen soon swam aboard, and took care of our bags for us. Some of us thought it better to wear two shirts, but as soon as we got to the French ship, one of them was taken away.

Captain Lejoille, of *Le Généreux*, was a great scoundrel, and used our captain like a brute. His men in the *Leander* stole the doctor's instruments when he was going to dress the men's wounds; for the wounded men were all left aboard, and Captain Lejoille kept the doctor from coming aboard the French ship to our captain, who was badly wounded. We had nothing but oil and rice to eat, and they made us work and refit the ship. We fished his foremast (another shot would have knocked it down), and knotted all his shrouds, for which Captain Lejoille promised us our liberty as soon as we got to Corfu; but as soon as we had done all the work, he started us down below, and kept us close till we got there. But we can't wonder at their being a little matter spiteful – see what a thrashing they got at the Nile![37]

The despatches that had been carried by Berry were at the bottom of the sea. The duplicates, sent by Naples, were on their slow way across Europe towards an England criss-crossed with rumours, first of a defeat for Nelson, then of a victory. In London, the First Lord had to defend Nelson's competence.

The victor of the Nile reached Naples on 22nd September, where he received a hero's welcome. Boats came out to Vanguard *carrying Sir William and Lady Hamilton, and King Ferdinand.*

Nelson described the scene in a letter to his wife:

The scene in the boat appeared terribly affecting. Up flew her

Ladyship and exclaiming: 'OH GOD IS IT POSSIBLE!' fell into
my arm more dead than alive. Tears however soon set matters
to rights, when alongside came the King. He took me by the hand,
calling me his deliverer and preserver, with every other expression
of kindness. In short all Naples calls me *Nostra Liberatore*, for the
scene with the lower classes was truly affecting. I hope one day to
have the pleasure of introducing you to Lady Hamilton. She is one
of the very best women in this world.[27]

Emma Hamilton had fainted on hearing news of Nelson's victory.

The effect was a shot. She fell apparently dead and is not yet
properly recovered from severe bruises.[27]

*The Queen of Naples had also fainted on hearing the news. And so
did Lord Spencer, in London, flat on his face, when the extent of the
Nile victory at last reached him.*

*It took Lieutenant Capel two months and a day to reach London
with the duplicate despatches. Within hours, salvos of guns were being
fired in the parks, and church bells were ringing. In a theatre, the
audience rose to their feet and sang* Rule Britannia. *Artists of every
kind wet their brushes, eager to depict the new national hero.*

Lady Hamilton wrote to Nelson, again at sea:

If I was a King of England, I would make you the most noble,
puissant Duke Nelson, Marquis Nile, Earl Alexandria, Viscount
Pyramid, Baron Crocodile and Prince Victory, that posterity might
have you in all forms.[27]

*In fact, on 6th October, he became Lord Nelson of the Nile and
Burnham Thorpe, with a pension for life of £2,000 a year. It was
as much as a junior naval officer could reasonably expect, but Nelson
pondered how St Vincent had become an Earl following his victory
on St Valentine's day, 1797, and Duncan had become a Viscount
after Camperdown. He complained to the knighted Berry that their
respective honours were 'proof how much more a battle fought near
England is prized to one fought at a great distance'.*

*Certainly the Nile victory was the greatest then achieved by the
British Navy – and the first major set-back for Napoleon, one that
was to enter his reflections again and again in defeat and exile.*

The Battle of Copenhagen

2 April 1801

*The glorious 2nd of April – a day when the
greatest dangers of navigation were overcome,
and the Danish force (which they thought
impregnable) totally taken or destroyed by
the consummate skill of the commanders and
by the undaunted bravery of as gallant a
band as ever defended the rights of this country.*
Nelson.

British Ships at the Battle of Copenhagen

LORD NELSON'S DIVISION

Elephant (flag)	74 guns	Vice-Admiral Lord Nelson
		Captain Thomas Foley
Defiance	74 guns	Rear-Admiral Thomas Graves
		Captain R. Ratalick
Edgar	74 guns	Captain George Murray
Bellona (grounded)	74 guns	Captain Sir T. Thompson
Ganges	74 guns	Captain Thomas Fremantle
Russell (grounded)	74 guns	Captain W. Cuming
Monarch	74 guns	Captain J. R. Mosse (killed)
Ardent	64 guns	Captain T. Bertie
Agamemnon (grounded)	64 guns	Captain F. D. Fancourt
Polyphemus	64 guns	Captain J. Lawford
Glatton	56 guns	Captain William Bligh
Isis	50 guns	Captain J. Walker

FRIGATES

Desirée	40 guns	Captain H. Inman
Amazon	38 guns	Captain Edward Riou (killed)
Blanche	36 guns	Captain G. E. Hamond
Alcmene	32 guns	Captain Samuel Sutton

SLOOPS

Dart	30 guns	Captain J. F. Devonshire
Arrow	30 guns	Captain W. Bolton
Cruiser	18 guns	Captain James Brisbane
Harpy	18 guns	Captain W. Birchall

BOMB VESSELS

Discovery	16 guns	Captain John Conn
Zebra	16 guns	Captain E. S. Clay
Sulphur	10 guns	Captain H. Whitter
Hecla	10 guns	Captain R. Hatherill
Explosion	8 guns	Captain J. H. Martin
Terror	8 guns	Captain S. C. Rowley
Volcano	8 guns	Captain J. Watson

FIRE SHIPS

Otter	14 guns	Captain G. M'Kinley
Zephyr	14 guns	Captain C. Upton

In addition Captain J. Rose, *Jamaica*, 26 guns, had command of six gun brigs which were to have raked the southernmost ships of the Danish line, had the current permitted.

SIR HYDE PARKER'S DIVISION

Defence, Ramillies, Veteran, Saturn, London, Warrior, St George, Raisonnable

In maintaining ascendancy at sea, British seamen were boarding and searching ships from neutral countries carrying goods to the enemy. Inevitably there were incidents, with heated diplomatic exchanges to follow.

One such incident occurred in December 1799 when a Danish frigate, escorting merchantmen, fired on British boats off Gibraltar. Relations between the British and Danish governments became even further strained when the following July British ships were in action with the Danish frigate Freja, *capturing it and seizing her convoy of six vessels. They were returned to the Danes on 29 August 1800. Two days before, referring to the* Freja *incident, Tsar Paul of Russia had called on the sovereigns of Denmark, Sweden, and Prussia to join him in a coalition of Armed Neutrality, which they did.*

The British government decided the time had come to send a strong fleet into the Baltic. Appointed Commander-in-Chief was Sir Hyde Parker, a rather pedestrian officer without the qualities the mission required. And a man with less tactical flair and knowledge (though twenty years senior) than his second in command – Lord Nelson, promoted to vice-admiral on New Year's Day, 1801.

The call for the Baltic operation came as a relief to Nelson. In England he had been fêted as 'the hero of the Nile' wherever he went; but his family and private life imposed severe strain. He had separated from his wife, and Emma Hamilton, whom he loved wildly, was carrying his child. He thankfully hoisted his flag on the captured San Josef *at Plymouth on 13th January, changing to the* St George *on his way to rendezvous with Sir Hyde Parker at Great Yarmouth.*

Six-hundred troops had embarked, under command of Lieutenant-Colonel the Hon. William Stewart. Stewart was in his twenties, and his youthful, patriotic ardour appealed to Nelson. His account of the Battle of Copenhagen is more detailed, and better written, than Colonel Drinkwater's description of St Vincent.

We entered Yarmouth Roads on March 6 or 7. The *St George* was the first three-decker which had so done. The flag of Sir Hyde Parker, the Commander-in-Chief, was flying on board one of the ships of the station, but was removed to the *London* on her arrival next day. Sir Hyde was on shore, and I remember that Lord Nelson regretted this. He reported his arrival, and his intention of waiting on him the next morning. We breakfasted that morning, as usual, soon after six o'clock, for we were always up before daylight. We went on shore, so as to be at Sir Hyde's door by eight o'clock, Lord Nelson choosing to be amusingly exact to that hour, which he considered a very late one for business.

Lord Nelson's plan would have been to have proceeded with the utmost dispatch, and with such ships as were in readiness, to the mouth of Copenhagen Harbour; then and there to have insisted on amity or war, and have brought the objects of negotiation to a speedy decision. He would have left orders for the remainder of the fleet to have followed in succession, as they were ready, and by the rapidity of his proceedings have anticipated the formidable preparations for defence which the Danes had scarcely thought of at that early season. The delay in Yarmouth Roads did not accord with his views.

An order from the Admiralty arrived on March 11, in consequence of which the fleet put to sea on the succeeding day. The land troops were equally distributed on board the line of battle ships, and I, repairing to the *London*, had not an opportunity of being with Lord Nelson, until our arrival off the sound. Our fleet consisted of about fifty sail; of these forty were pendants, sixteen being of the line.

On the 15th, we encountered a heavy gale, which in some measure scattered the fleet, and prevented our reaching the Naze until the 18th. On the next day, when off the Scaw, the whole were nearly collected; a north-west wind blew, and an opportunity appeared to have been lost of proceeding through the Cattegat. Every delay, however, trifling, gave cause for regret, and favoured the views of the Northern Coalition.

The openness of those seas had rarely been equalled at this season of the year, and in particular called for activity in our movements. The Commander-in-Chief had probably, however, instructions by which he acted; and if so, this, in addition to numerous instances of a similar nature, proves the propriety of discretionary powers, whenever success is to depend on energy and activity. Lord Nelson was, as I understand, greatly vexed at the delay.

On the 21st it blew hard, and we anchored for twenty-four hours.[38]

That day Nelson attended a Council of War on board the London, *and the following day penned to his Commander-in-Chief one of his best letters:*

My dear Sir Hyde,

The conversation we had yesterday has naturally, from its importance, been the subject of my thoughts; and the more I have reflected, the more I am confirmed in opinion, that not a moment should be lost in attacking the enemy. They will every day and hour be stronger; we shall never be so good a match for them as at this moment.

The only consideration in my mind is how to get at them with the least risk to our ships. By Mr Vansittart's [negotiating diplomat] account, the Danes have taken every means in their power to prevent our getting to attack Copenhagen by the Passage of the Sound. Cronenburg has been strengthened, the Crown Islands fortified, on the outermost of which there are twenty guns pointing mostly downwards, and only eight hundred yards from very formidable batteries placed under the Citadel supported by five sail of the line, seven floating batteries of fifty guns each, besides small-craft, gun-boats, etc., etc. And that the Revel Squadron of twelve or fourteen sail of the line are soon expected as also five sail of Swedes.

It would appear by what you have told me of your instructions, that Government took for granted you would find no difficulty in getting off Copenhagen, and in the event of a failure of negotiation, you might instantly attack; and that there would be scarcely a doubt but the Danish Fleet would be destroyed, and the capital made so hot that Denmark would listen to reason and its true interest. By Mr Vansittart's account, their state of preparation exceeds what he conceives our government thought possible, and that the Danish government is hostile to us in the greatest possible degree.

Therefore here you are, with almost the safety, certainly with the honour of England more entrusted to you than ever yet fell to any British officer. On your decision depends, whether our country shall be degraded in the eyes of Europe, or whether she shall rear her head higher than ever: again do I repeat, never did our country depend so much on the success of any fleet as on this. How best to honour our country and abate the pride of her enemies, by defeating their schemes, must be the subject of your deepest considerations as commander-in-chief; and if what I have to offer can be the least useful in forming your decision, you are most heartily welcome.

I shall begin with supposing you are determined to enter by the Passage of the Sound, as there are those who think, if you are to leave that Passage open, that the Danish fleet may sail from Copenhagen, and join the Dutch or French. I own I have no fears on that subject; for it is not likely that whilst their capital is menaced with an attack, 9,000 of her best men should be sent out of the Kingdom. I suppose that some damage may arise amongst our masts and yards; yet, perhaps there will not be one of them but could be made serviceable again. You are now about Cronenburg: if the wind be fair, and you determine to attack the ships and Crown Islands, you must expect the natural issue of such a battle – ships crippled, and perhaps one or two lost; for the wind which carries you in will most probably not bring out a crippled ship. The mode I call taking the bull by the horns. It, however, will not prevent the Revel Ships, or Swedes, from joining the Danes; and to prevent this from taking effect, is in my humble opinion, a measure absolutely necessary – and still to attack Copenhagen.

Two modes are in my view; one to pass Cronenburg, taking the risk of damage, and to pass up the deepest and straightest channel above the Middle Grounds; and coming down the Garbar or King's Channel, to attack their floating batteries, etc., etc., as we find it convenient. It must have the effect of preventing a junction between the Russians, Swedes and Danes, and may give us an opportunity of bombarding Copenhagen. I am also pretty certain that a passage could be found to the northward of Southholm for all our ships; perhaps it might be necessary to warp a short distance in the very narrow part.

Should this mode of attack be ineligible, the passage of the Belt, I have no doubt, would be accomplished in four or five days, and then the attack by Draco could be carried into effect, and the junction of the Russians prevented, with every probability of success against the Danish floating batteries. What effect a bombardment might have, I am not called upon to give an opinion; but think the way should be cleared for the trial.

Supposing us through the Belt, with the wind first westerly, would it not be possible to either go with the fleet, or detach ten ships of three and two decks, with one bomb and two fire-ships, to Revel, to destroy the Russian squadron at that place? I do not see the great risk of such a detachment, and with the remainder to attempt the business at Copenhagen. The measure may be thought bold, but I am of opinion the boldest measures are the safest; and our country demands a most vigorous exertion of her force, directed with judgment. In supporting you, my dear Sir Hyde, through the arduous and important task you have undertaken, no exertion of head or heart shall be wanting from your most obedient and faithful servant.

Nelson and Brontë*.[6]

Stewart:

Lord Nelson was impatient for action . . . his object was to go to Copenhagen, and he said, 'Let it be by the Sound, by the Belt, or anyhow, only lose not an hour.' On the 26th the whole fleet sailed for the Great Belt; but after proceeding for a few leagues along the coast of Zealand, the plan was suddenly changed.[38]

Ralfe's Naval Biography *says that following the Council of War,*

---

*The dukedom of Brontë was conferred on Nelson by the King of Naples in 1800.

Admiral Sir Robert Walker Otway, Flag-Captain, persuaded Sir Hyde Parker that the navigational risks of the Belt made the Sound the preferable approach to Copenhagen.

As if a more than sufficient time had not been given for the Danes to prepare their defence [Stewart fretted], another message was sent, on March 27, to the Governor of Elsinore, Stricker, to discover his intentions relative to opposing our fleet, if it were to pass the sound.[38]

Admiral Sir Hyde Parker's Journal:

Saturday, March 28. p.m. – Moderate and cloudy. Ordered Captain Murray of the *Edgar* to take the bomb-vessels under his protection, and proceed and anchor off within a distance of Cronenburg and Elsinore Castle, prepare for bombardment, but not to fire or bombard those places unless attacked, but wait for my coming up. At three, they sailed.

At midnight, Captain Brisbane brought on board an officer from Copenhagen, with a letter from the Governor of Cronenburg Castle, informing me he is not allowed to let a fleet whose intentions is not yet known to approach the cannon of the castle he has the honour to command, but if I have any proposals to make, the King of Denmark wishes to have a determined answer before the fleet approaches nearer.

Sunday, March 29. a.m. – Returned for answer, that finding the intentions of Denmark hostile to his Britannic Majesty, I consider his letter as a declaration of war, and I therefore shall no longer refrain from hostilities.[31]

Stewart:

On March 26, the *Elephant*, and another seventy-four, had joined the fleet, bringing the melancholy intelligence of the loss of the *Invincible*, 74-guns, Rear-Admiral Totty, Captain Rennie, one of our squadron, on the sandbank called Hammond's Knowl. On the 29th, Lord Nelson shifted his flag from the *St George* to the *Elephant*, commanded by his intimate friend, Captain Foley, in order to carry on operations in a lighter ship. Both the 28th and 29th were unfortunately calm: orders had, however, been given for the fleet to pass through the Sound as soon as the wind should permit.

At daylight, on the morning of the 30th, it blew a topsail breeze from N.W. The signal was made, and the fleet proceeded in the order of battle previously arranged: Lord Nelson's division in the van, the Commander-in-Chief's in the centre, and Admiral Grave's in the rear. Captain Murray in the *Edgar*, with the fleet of bomb and gun vessels, took their station off Cronenburg Castle on the preceding morning; and, upon the first Danish shot, opened their fire upon the castle.

The semi-circular form of the land off Elsinore, which was thickly lined with batteries, caused our fleet to pass in a form truly picturesque, and nearly similar. It had been our intention to have kept in mid-channel; the forbearance of the Swedes not having been counted upon, the lighter vessels were on the larboard side of our line of battle, and were to have engaged the Helsinburg shore: not a shot, however, was fired, nor any batteries apparent, and our fleet inclined accordingly to that side, so as completely to avoid the Danish shot which fell in showers, but at least a cable's length from our ships.

The Danish batteries opened a fire, as we understood, of nearly one hundred pieces of cannon and mortars, as soon as our leading ship, the *Monarch*, came abreast of them; and they continued in one uninterrupted blaze during the passage of the fleet, to the no small amusement of our crews, none of whom received injury, except from the bursting of one of our guns. Some of our leading ships at first returned a few rounds, but, perceiving the minutility, desisted. The whole came to anchor about mid-day, between the island of Huen and Copenhagen; the division under Captain Murray following, as soon as the main body had passed. As is usually the case in sea bombardments, little or no damage was afterwards found to have been done by our shells.

Our fleet was no sooner at anchor, than the Commander-in-Chief, accompanied by Lord Nelson, two or three senior captains, the commanding officer of the artillery and of the troops, proceeded in a schooner to reconnoitre the harbour and channels. We soon perceived that our delay had been of important advantage to the enemy, who had lined the northern edge of the shoals near the

Crown batteries, and the front of the harbour and arsenal, with a formidable flotilla. The Trekroner battery appeared, in particular, to have been strengthened, and all the buoys of the Northern and of the King's Channels had been removed. Having examined these points with some attention, the party returned to the *London*.

The night of March 30 was employed by some of the intelligent masters and pilots, under the direction of Captain Brisbane, in ascertaining the channels round the great shoal called the Middle Ground, and in laying down fresh buoys, the Danes having either removed or misplaced the former ones.

On the next day, the Commander-in-Chief and Lord Nelson, attended, as before, with the addition of all the artillery officers, proceeded in the *Amazon* frigate, Captain Riou, to the examination of the Northern channel, and of the flotilla from the eastward. Captain Riou became on this occasion first known to Lord Nelson, who was struck with admiration at the superior discipline and seamanwhip that were observable on board the *Amazon* during the proceedings of this day.

The Danish line of defence was formed in a direct line eastward from the Trekroner battery, and extended at least two miles along the coast of Amak: it was ascertained to consist of the hulls of seven line-of-battle ships with jury masts, two only being fully rigged, ten pontoons or floating batteries, one bomb-ship rigged, and two or three smaller craft. On the Trekroner, appeared to be nearly seventy guns; on the smaller battery, in-shore, six or seven guns; and on the coast of Amak, several batteries which were within a long range of the King's Channel. Off the harbour's mouth, which was to the westward of the Trekroner, were moored four line of battle ships and a frigate; two of the former and the latter were fully rigged. Their whole line of defence, from one extreme point to the other, might embrace an extent of nearly four miles. The dockyard and arsenal were in line nearly south, within the Trekroner, about half a mile distant.

A few shot were fired at the *Amazon* whenever we approached the leading ship of their line. The officers of artillery were desired to ascertain, whether, in the event of the line of defence being in part or wholly removed, they could place their bomb-ships, of which there were seven, so as to play with effect on the dockyards and arsenal. After some hours' survey, the *Amazon* returned to the fleet, when the opinions of the artillery officers were given in the affirmative, if the flotilla to the eastward of the Crown batteries were only removed.

A Council of War was held in the afternoon, and the mode which might be advisable for the attack was considered: that from the eastward appeared to be preferred. Lord Nelson offered his services, requiring ten line of battle ships, and the whole of the smaller craft. The Commander-in-Chief, with sound discretion, and in a handsome manner, not only left everything to Lord Nelson for this detached service, but gave two more line of battle ships than he demanded.

During this Council of War, the energy of Lord Nelson's character was remarked: certain difficulties had been started by some of the members, relative to each of the three powers we should either have to engage, in succession or united, in those seas. The number of the Russians was, in particular, represented as formidable. Lord Nelson kept pacing the cabin, mortified at everything which savoured either of alarm or irresolution. When the above remark was applied to the Swedes, he sharply observed, 'The more numerous the better;' and when to the Russians, he repeatedly said, 'So much the better. I wish they were twice as many; the easier the victory, depend on it.' He alluded, as he afterwards explained in private, to the total want of tactique among the Northern Fleets; and to his intention, whenever he should bring either the Swedes or Russians to action, of attacking the head of their line, and confusing their movements as much as possible. He used to say, 'Close with a Frenchman, but out-manoeuvre a Russian.

The night of the 31st was employed, as the preceding, in ascertaining, even by buoy lights, the course of the upper channel.

On the afternoon of April 1, the whole fleet removed to an anchorage within two leagues of the town, off the N.W. end of the Middle Ground. It was intended that the division under Lord

Nelson should proceed from this point through the Northern Channel.

His Lordship, accompanied by a few chosen friends, made his last observations during that morning on board the *Amazon*, and about one o'clock returning to the *Elephant*, he threw out the wished-for signal to weigh. The shout with which it was received throughout the division was heard to a considerable distance; the ships then weighed, and followed the *Amazon* in succession through the narrow channel. The wind was light, but favourable, and not one accident occurred. The buoys were accurately laid down, and the smaller craft distinctly pointed out the course: the gallant Riou led the way – the scene was perfect.

About dark, the whole fleet was at its anchorage off Draco point; the headmost of the enemy's line not more than two miles distant. The small extent of the anchoring-ground, as the fleet did not consist of less than thirty-three pendants, caused the ships to be so much crowded, which the calmness of the evening increased, that had the enemy but taken due advantage of it by shells from mortar-boats, or from Amak Island, the greatest mischief might have ensured. They threw two or three about eight p.m., which served to show that we were within range. The Danes were, however, too much occupied during this night in manning their ships, and strengthening their line; not from immediate expectation, as we afterwards learned, of our attack – conceiving the channel impracticable to so large a fleet – but as a precaution against our nearer approach. Our guard-boats were actively employed between us and the enemy, and Captain Hardy even rowed to their leading ship; sounding round her, and using a pole when he was apprehensive of being heard. His chief object was to ascertain the bearing of the eastern end of the Middle Ground – the greatest obstacle, as it proved, that we had to contend with.[38]

Nelson's character is further revealed in Stewart's description of the eve of battle activities on board the Elephant:

As soon as the fleet was at anchor, the gallant Nelson sat down to table with a large party of his comrades in arms. He was in the highest spirits, and drank to a leading wind, and to the success of the ensuing day. Captains Foley, Hardy, Fremantle, Riou, Inman, his Lordship's second in command, Admiral Graves, and a few others to whom he was particularly attached, were of this interesting party; from which every man separated with feelings of admiration for their great leader, and with anxious impatience to follow him to the approaching battle. The signal to prepare for battle had been made early in the evening.

All the captains retired to their respective ships, Riou excepted, who with Lord Nelson and Foley arranged the order of battle, and those instructions that were to be issued to each ship on the succeeding day.

From the previous fatigue of this day, and of the two preceding, Lord Nelson was so much exhausted while dictating his instructions, that it was recommended to him by us all, and, indeed, insisted upon by his old servant, Allen, who assumed much command on these occasions, that he should go to his cot. It was placed on the floor, but from it he still continued to dictate.

Captain Hardy returned about eleven, and reported the practicability of the channel, and the depth of water up to the ships of the enemy's line.

The orders were completed about one o'clock, when half a dozen clerks in the foremost cabin proceeded to transcribe them. Lord Nelson's impatience again showed itself; for instead of sleeping undisturbedly, as he might have done, he was every half hour calling from his cot to these clerks to hasten their work, for that the wind was becoming fair: he was constantly receiving a report of this during the night. Their work being finished about six in the morning, his Lordship, who was previously up and dressed, breakfasted, and about seven made the signal for all captains. The instructions were delivered to each by eight o'clock; and a special command was given to Captain Riou to act as circumstances might require. The land-forces and a body of five-hundred seamen were to have been united under the command of Captain Fremantle and the Honourable Colonel Stewart, and as soon as the fire of the Crown Battery should be silenced, they were to storm the work and destroy it. The division under the Commander-in-Chief was to menace the ships at the entrance of the harbour; the intricacy of the channel would, however, have prevented their entering. Captain Murray in the *Edgar* was to lead.[38]

ORDERS FOR THE ATTACK

As Vice-Admiral Lord Nelson cannot with precision mark the situation of the different descriptions of the enemy's floating batteries and smaller vessels, lying between their two-decked ships and hulks, the ships which are to be opposed to the floating batteries, etc., etc., will find their stations by observing the stations of the ships to be opposed to the two-decker ships and hulks.

LINE OF BATTLE

These ships are to fire in passing on to their stations.	{	*Edgar* *Ardent* *Glatton* *Isis* *Agamemnon*	}	Are to lead in succession.

The *Edgar* to anchor abreast of No. 5. The *Ardent* to pass the *Edgar*, and anchor abreast of Nos. 6 and 7. The *Glatton* to pass the *Ardent*, and anchor abreast of No. 9. *The Isis* to anchor abreast of No. 2. The *Agamemnon* to anchor abreast of No. 1.

	Bellona *Elephant* *Ganges* *Monarch* *Defiance* *Russell* *Polyphemus*	}	To take their station and anchor, as is prescribed by the following arrangement.

Memorandum – No. 1 begins with the enemy's first ship to the southward.

No.	Rate	Supposed number of guns mounted on one side	Station of the Line as they are to anchor and engage
1	74	28	{ *Agamemnon.* *Désiré* is to follow *Agamemnon*, and rake No. 2.

No.	Rate	Supposed number of guns mounted on one side	Station of the Line as they are to anchor and engage
2	64	26	*Isis.*
3	Low floating batteries,	10	It is hoped the *Désirée's* fire will not only rake No. 1, but also rake these two floating batteries. Capt. Rose is to place the six gun-brigs so as to rake them also.
4	ship-rigged, rather lay within the Line	10	
5	64	27	*Edgar.*
6	Pontoon	10	*Ardent.*
7	Frigate hulk	12	
8	Small – no guns visible		*Glatton.*
9	64	20	
10	Ship gun-boat of 22 guns	11	*Bellona*, to give her attention to support the *Glatton.*
11	Pontoons, or	12	
12	floating batteries	12	
13	74	36	*Elephant.*
14	Pontoons, or	12	*Ganges.*
15	floating batteries	12	
16	64	30	*Monarch.*
17	64	30	*Defiance.*
18	64	30	*Russell.*
19	64	30	*Polyphemus.*
20	A small ship, supposed a bomb	11	

The six gun-boats, Captain Rose is to place with the *Jamaica*, to make a raking fire upon No. 1. The gun-boats, it is presumed, may get far enough astern of No. 1, to rake Nos. 3 and 4; and Captain Rose is to advance with the ship and vessels under his orders, to the northward, as he may perceive the British fire to cease where he is first stationed.

Nos. 1, 2, 3, and 4, being subdued, which is expected to happen at an early period, the *Isis* and *Agamemnon* are to cut their cables, and immediately make sail and take their station ahead of the *Polyphemus*, in order to support that part of the line. One flat boat, manned and armed, is to remain upon the off side of each line of battle ship. The remaining flat boats, with the boats for boarding, which will be sent by Admiral Sir Hyde Parker under the command of the First Lieutenant of the *London*, are to keep as near to the *Elephant* as possible, but out of the line of fire, and to be ready to receive the directions of Lord Nelson.

The four launches with anchors and cables, which will be sent by Admiral Sir Hyde Parker, under the command of a lieutenant of the *London*, to be as near to the *Elephant* as possible, out of the line of fire, ready to receive orders from Vice-Admiral Lord Nelson.

The *Alcmene, Blanche, Arrow, Dart, Zephyr*, and *Otter* fire-ships, are to proceed under the orders of Captain Riou, of the *Amazon*, to perform such service as he is directed by Lord Nelson.[24]

At daybreak the wind was announced as becoming perfectly fair. Between 8.00 and 9.00 a.m. the pilots and masters were summoned on board the Elephant.

A most unpleasant degree of hesitation prevailed amongst them all [Stewart reported] when they came to the point about the bearing of the east end of the Middle Ground, and about the exact line of deep water in the King's Channel. Not a moment was to be lost; the wind was fair, and the signal made for action. Lord Nelson urged them to be steady, to be resolute, and to decide.[38]

Afterwards Nelson was to speak bitterly of this moment: 'I experienced in the Sound the misery of having the honour of our country intrusted to a set of pilots, who have no other thought than to keep the ships clear of danger, and their own silly heads clear of shot.'

At length Mr Briarley, the master of the *Bellona*, declared himself prepared to lead the fleet [Stewart continues]. His example was quickly followed by the rest. They repaired on board their respective ships, and at half-past nine the signal was given to weigh in succession.[38]

The battle opened calamitously for the British. Nelson was repeating an attack on ships at anchor on lines similar to those which had proved successful at Aboukir Bay. At Copenhagen there were early set-backs.

Stewart tells us that the signal to weigh:

... was quickly obeyed by the *Edgar*, who proceeded in a noble manner for the channel. The *Agamemnon* was to follow, but happened to take a course in a direct line for the end of the shoal. The *Polyphemus*' signal, Captain Lawford, was then made, and this change in the order of sailing was promptly executed. The *Edgar* was, however, unsupported for a considerable time; when within range of the *Provestein*, she was fired at, but returned not a shot until she was nearly opposite to the number which was destined for her by the instructions – she then poured in her broadsides with great effect.

The *Polyphemus* was followed by the *Isis*, *Bellona*, and *Russell;* the former, commanded by Captain Walker, took her station most gallantly, and had the severest birth this day of any ship, the *Monarch* perhaps not excepted. The *Bellona* and *Russell*, in going down the channel, kept too close on the starboard shoal, and ran aground; they were, however, within range of shot, and continued to fire with much spirit upon such of the enemy's ships as they could reach.

An instance of Lord Nelson's presence of mind now occurred: – In going down the channel (the water was supposed to shoal on the larboard shore), each ship had been ordered to pass her leader on the starboard side. When it came to the turn of the *Elephant*, his Lordship, thinking that the two above-mentioned ships had kept too far in that direction, made the signal to close with the enemy. Perceiving that this was not done, which their being aground unknown to him was the cause of, he ordered the *Elephant*'s helm to starboard, quitted the intended order of sailing, and went within those ships. The same course was consequently followed by the succeeding ships, and the major part of our fleet might thus, in all probability, have been saved from going on shore. In succession, as each ship arrived nearly opposite to her number in the Danish line, she let her anchor go by the stern, the wind nearly aft, and presented her broadside to the enemy.

The action began at five minutes past ten. In about half an hour afterwards, the first half of our fleet was engaged, and before half past eleven, the battle became general.

The *Elephant*'s station was in the centre, opposite to the Danish Commodore, who commanded in the *Dannebrog*, 62 guns. Our distance was nearly a cable's length, and this was the average distance at which the action was fought; its being so great, caused the long duration of it. Lord Nelson was most anxious to get nearer; but the same error which had led the two ships on the shoal induced our master and pilots to dread shoaling their water on the larboard shore: they, therefore, when the lead was a quarter less five, refused to approach nearer, and insisted on the anchor being let go. We afterwards found that had we but approached the enemy's line, we should have deepened our water up to their very side, and closed with them: as it was, the *Elephant* engaged in little more than four fathom.

The *Glatton* had her station immediately astern of us; the *Ganges*, *Monarch*, and *Defiance* ahead; the distance between each not exceeding a half cable. The judgment with which each ship calculated her station in that intricate channel was admirable throughout. The failure of the three ships that were aground, and whose force was to have been opposed to the Trekroner battery, left this day, as glorious for seamanship as for courage, incomplete. The lead was in many ships confided to the master alone; and the contest that arose on board the *Elephant*, which of the two officers who attended the heaving of it should stand in the larboard chains, was a noble competition, and greatly pleased the heart of Nelson, as he paced the quarter deck.

The gallant Riou, perceiving the blank in the original plan for the attack of the Crown Battery, proceeded down the line with his squadron of frigates, and attempted, but in vain, to fulfil the duties of the absent ships of the line. His force was unequal to it.

About one p.m., few if any of the enemy's heavy ships and praams* had ceased to fire. The *Isis* had greatly suffered by the superior weight of the *Provestein*'s fire; and if it had not been for the judicious diversion of it by the *Désirée*, who raked her, and for other assistance from the *Polyphemus*, the *Isis* would have been destroyed. Both the *Isis* and *Bellona* had received injury by the

* Flat-bottomed boats mounted with guns.

bursting of some of their guns. The *Monarch* was also suffering severely under the united fire of the *Holstein* and *Zealand;* and only two of our bomb-vessels could get to their station on the Middle Ground, and open their mortars on the arsenal, directing their shells over both fleets. Our squadron of gun-brigs, impeded by currents, could not, with one exception, although commanded by Captain Rose in the *Jamaica*, weather the eastern end of the Middle Ground, or come into action. The division of the Commander-in-Chief acted according to the preconcerted plan; but could only menace the entrance to the harbour. The *Elephant* was warmly engaged by the *Dannebrog*, and by two heavy praams on her bow and quarter. Signals of distress were on board the *Bellona* and *Russell*, and of inability from the *Agamemnon*. The contest, in general, although from the relaxed state of the enemy's fire, it might not have given much room for apprehension as to the result, had certainly at one p.m., not declared itself in favour of either side.

About this juncture, and in this posture of affairs, the signal was thrown out on board the *London*, for the action to cease.[38]

Admiral Sir Hyde Parker actually made the signal at 1.30 p.m., but he would have made it half an hour earlier, had not his Flag-Captain, Admiral Sir Robert Walker Otway, pleaded that first he be allowed to go on board the Elephant *and discover how things were at the centre of the battle. From the* London, *about four miles to leeward, it seemed to the Commander-in-Chief that the attack had been a disastrous failure: two British ships had grounded, one had failed to weather the shoals at the entrance to the channel, and those engaged were being subjected to a fierce fire from the Danish batteries that refused to be checked. Before Otway could reach Nelson, Sir Hyde's nerve broke, and he made the signal for retreat.*

How Nelson reacted, Stewart now tells us:

Lord Nelson was at this time, as he had been during the whole action, walking the starboard side of the quarter-deck; sometimes much animated, and at others heroically fine in his observations. A shot through the mainmast knocked a few splinters about us. He observed to me, with a smile, 'It is warm work, and this day may be the last to any of us at a moment;' and then stopping short at the gangway, he used an expression never to be erased from my memory, and said with emotion, 'but mark you, I would not be elsewhere for thousands.'

When the signal, No. 39, was made, the Signal-Lieutenant reported it to him. He continued his walk, and did not appear to take notice of it. The Lieutenant meeting his Lordship at the next turn asked whether he should repeat it? Lord Nelson answered, 'No, acknowledge it.' On the officer returning to the poop, his Lordship called after him, 'Is No. 16 [for close action] still hoisted?' The Lieutenant answering in the affirmative, Lord Nelson said, 'Mind you keep it so.'

He now walked the deck considerably agitated, which was always known by his moving the stump of his right arm. After a turn or two, he said to me, in a quick manner, 'Do you know what's shown on board of the Commander-in-Chief, No. 39?' On asking him what that meant, he answered, 'Why, to leave off action.' 'Leave off action!' he repeated, and then added, with a shrug, 'Now, damn me if I do.' He also observed, I believe, to Captain Foley, 'You know, Foley, I have only one eye – I have a right to be blind sometimes;' and then with an archness peculiar to his character, putting the glass to his blind eye, he exclaimed, 'I really do not see the signal.'

This remarkable signal was, therefore, only acknowledged on board the *Elephant*, not repeated. Admiral Graves did the latter, not being able to distinguish the *Elephant*'s conduct. Either by a fortunate accident, or intentionally, No. 16 was not displaced.[38]

As at St Vincent, though in different circumstances and manner, Nelson disobeyed the orders of his Commander-in-Chief. He had done so at St Vincent because he had spotted what was necessary; success justified the act of disobedience. Now he saw clearly that Parker's decision was a wrong one, made at too great a distance from the battle, so that he could not see signs that the Danish resistance was at last beginning to weaken. Further: an attempted withdrawal past the powerful Trekroner batteries would have led to a calamitious loss of ships and men. Thus judgement and character united splendidly in

Nelson's quick decision to 'turn a blind eye' to his Commander-in-Chief's order.

Captain Riou obeyed the order, and it cost him his life. He had been given a free hand by Nelson, and on seeing the upset to the agreed order of attack, caused by the misfortunes to the Agamemnon, Bellona, *and* Russell, *he had fearlessly taken his squadron of lightly-armed frigates into an attack on the Trekroner batteries.*

The squadron of frigates obeyed the signal [No. 39], and hauled off [continues Stewart]. That brave officer, Captain Riou, was killed by a raking shot, when the *Amazon* showed her stern to the Trekroner. He was sitting on a gun, was encouraging his men, and had been wounded in the head by a splinter. He had expressed himself grieved at being thus obliged to retreat, and nobly observed, 'What will Nelson think of us?' His clerk was killed by his side; and by another shot, several of the marines, while hauling on the main-brace, shared the same fate. Riou then exclaimed, 'Come then, my boys, let us all die together!' The words were scarcely uttered, when the fatal shot severed him in two.[38]

Nelson's reading of the battle was soon proved correct.

The action now continued with unabated vigour. About two p.m. the greater part of the Danish line had ceased to fire: some of the lighter ships were adrift, and the carnage on board of the enemy, who reinforced their crews from the shore, was dreadful. The taking possession of such ships as had struck, was, however, attended with difficulty; partly by reason of the batteries on Amak Island protecting them, and partly because an irregular fire was made on our boats, as they approached, from the ships themselves. The *Dannebrog* acted in this manner, and fired at our boat, although that ship was not only on fire and had struck, but the Commodore, Fischer, had removed his pendant, and had deserted her. A renewed attack on her by the *Elephant* and *Glatton*, for a quarter of an hour, not only completely silenced and disabled the *Dannebrog*, but, by the use of grape, nearly killed every man who was in the praams ahead and astern of that unfortunate ship. On our smoke clearing away, the *Dannebrog* was found to be drifting in flames before the wind, spreading terror throughout the enemy's lines. The usual lamentable scene then ensued; and our boats rowed in every direction to save the crew, who were throwing themselves from her at every port-hole; few, however, were left unwounded in her after our last broadsides, or could be saved. She drifted to leeward, and about half-past three blew up.[38]

Now came Nelson's second controversial act that day.

The time of half-past two brings me to a most important part of Lord Nelson's conduct on this day, and about which so much discussion has arisen: his sending a Flag of Truce on shore. To the best of my recollection, the facts were as follows.

After the *Dannebrog* was adrift, and had ceased to fire, the action was found to be over along the whole of the line astern of us; but not so with the ships ahead and with the Crown batteries. Whether from ignorance of the custom of war, or from confusion on board the prizes, our boats were, as before mentioned, repulsed from the ships themselves, or fired at from Amak Island. Lord Nelson naturally lost temper at this, and observed, 'That he must either send on shore, and stop this irregular proceeding, or send in our fire-ships and burn them.' He accordingly retired into the stern gallery, and wrote, with great dispatch, that well known letter addressed to the Crown Prince.

'To the Brothers of Englishmen, The Danes.

'Lord Nelson has directions to spare Denmark, when no longer resisting; but if the firing is continued on the part of Denmark, Lord Nelson will be obliged to set on fire all the floating-batteries he has taken, without having the power of saving the brave Danes who have defended them.

'Dated on board His Brittanic Majesty's ship *Elephant*, Copenhagen Roads, April 2nd, 1801.'

Nelson and Brontë, Vice-Admiral,

under the command of Admiral Sir Hyde Parker.[38]

Thomas Wallis, purser of the Elephant:

Lord Nelson wrote the note at the casing of the rudder-head, and as he wrote, I took a copy, both of us standing. The original was put into an envelope, and sealed with his Arms; at first I was going to seal it with a wafer, but he would not allow this to be done, observing that it must be sealed, or the enemy would think it was written and sent in a hurry.[27]

Colonel Stewart:

This letter was conveyed on shore through the contending fleets by Captain Sir Frederick Thesiger, who acted as his Lordship's Aid-de-camp; and found the Prince near the Sally-port, animating his people in a spirited manner.

Whether we were actually firing at that time in the *Elephant* or not, I am unable to recollect; it could only have been partially, at such of the farther ships as had not struck. The three ships ahead of us were, however, engaged; and from the superiority of the force opposed to them, it was by no means improbable that Lord Nelson's observing eye pointed out to him the expediency of a prudent conduct. Whether this suggested to him the policy of a Flag of Truce or not, two solid reasons were apparent, and were such as to justify the measure: viz., the necessity of stopping the irregular fire from the ships which had surrendered – and the singular opportunity that was thus given, of sounding the feelings of enemy, who had reluctantly entered into the war, and who must feel the generosity of the first offer of amity coming from a conquering foe. If there was a third reason for the conduct of the noble Admiral, and some of his own officers assert this, it was unnecessary that it should have been expressed; it was certainly not avowed, and will for ever remain a matter of conjecture.

While the boat was absent, the animated fire of the ships ahead of us, and the approach of two of the Commander-in-Chief's division, the *Ramillies* and *Defence*, caused the remainder of the enemy's line to the eastward of the Trekroner to strike: that formidable Work continued its fire, but fortunately at too long a range to do serious damage to any one except the *Monarch*, whose loss in men, this day, exceeded that of any line of battle during the war. From the uninjured state of this outwork, which had been manned at the close of the action with nearly 1,500 men, it was deemed impracticable to carry into execution the projected plan for storming it; the boats for this service had been on the starboard side of each ship during the action. The firing from the Crown battery and from our leading ships did not cease until past three o'clock, when the Danish Adjutant-General, Lindholm, returning with a Flag of Truce, directed the fire of the battery to be suspended. The signal for doing the same, on our part, was then made from our ship to those engaged. The action closed after five hours' duration, four of which were warmly contested.

The answer from the Prince Regent was to inquire more minutely into the purport of the message. I should here observe, that previous to the boat's getting on board, Lord Nelson had taken the opinion of his valuable friends, Fremantle and Foley, the former of whom had been sent for from the *Ganges*, as to the practicability of advancing with the ships which were least damaged, upon that part of the Danish line of defence yet uninjured. Their opinions were averse from it; and, on the other hand, decided in favour of removing our fleet, whilst the wind yet held fair, from their present intricate channel.

Lord Nelson was now prepared how to act when Mr Lindholm came on board, and the following answer was returned to the Crown Prince by Captain Sir Frederick Thesiger: 'Lord Nelson's object in sending the Flag of Truce was humanity; he therefore consents that hostilities shall cease, and that the wounded Danes may be taken on shore. And Lord Nelson will take his prisoners out of the vessels, and burn and carry off his prizes as he shall think fit. Lord Nelson, with humble duty to His Royal Highness the Prince of Denmark, will consider this the greatest victory he has ever gained, if it may be the cause of a happy reconciliation and union between his own most gracious Sovereign and His Majesty the King of Denmark.'

His Lordship, having finished this letter, referred the Adjutant-General to the Commander-in-Chief, who was at anchor at least four miles off, for a conference on the important points which the latter part of the message had alluded to; and to this General Lindholm did not object, but proceeded to the *London*. Lord Nelson wisely foresaw that, exclusive of the valuable opportunity that now offered itself for a renewal of Peace, time would be gained by this long row out to sea for our leading ships, which were much crippled, to clear the shoals, and whose course was under the immediate fire of the Trekroner.

The Adjutant-General was no sooner gone to the *London*, and Captain Thesiger despatched on shore than the signal was made for the *Glatton*, *Elephant*, *Ganges*, *Defiance*, and *Monarch*, to weigh in succession. The intricacy of the channel now showed the great utility of what had been done; the *Monarch*, as first ship, immediately hit on a shoal, but was pushed over it by the *Ganges* taking her amid-ships. The *Glatton* went clear, but the *Defiance* and *Elephant* ran aground, leaving the Crown Battery at a mile distance; and there they remained fixed, the former until ten o'clock that night, and the latter until eight, notwithstanding every exertion which their fatigued crews could make to relieve them. Had there been no cessation of hostilities, their situation would certainly have been perilous; but it should be observed, on the other hand, that measures would in that case have been adopted, and they were within our power, for destroying this formidable Work.

The *Elephant* being aground, Lord Nelson followed the Adjutant-General about four o'clock to the *London*, where that negotiation first began, which terminated in an honourable Peace. He was low in spirit at the surrounding scene of devastation, and particularly felt for the blowing up of the *Dannebrog*. 'Well!' he exclaimed, 'I have fought contrary to orders, and I shall perhaps be hanged: never mind, let them.'[38]

He need not have worried. As at St Vincent, success had justified his actions – and the greeting from his Commander-in-Chief was cordial.

Lindholm returned to Copenhagen the same evening [Stewart concludes], when it was agreed that all prizes should be surrendered, and the suspension of hostilities continue for twenty-four hours; the whole of the Danish wounded were to be received on shore.

Lord Nelson then repaired on board the *St George*, and the night was actively passed by the boats of the division which had not been engaged in getting afloat the ships that were ashore, and in bringing out the prizes.[38]

Colonel Stewart's narrative is by far the most valuable eye-witness account of the Battle of Copenhagen, combining a comprehensive description of the day's activities with many revealing pictures of Nelson on board the Elephant. *But once again we can turn to a midshipman on one of the British ships to discover how it was among the men most hotly engaged.*

As Stewart pointed out, the Monarch *took the heaviest punishment that day among Nelson's division, her Captain being one of the fatalities. Midshipman Millard survived, to write:*

The hammocks were piped up at six, but having had the middle watch I indulged myself with another nap, from which I was roused by the drum beating to quarters. I bustled on deck, examined the guns under my directions, saw them provided with hand-spikes, spare breechings, tackles, etc., and reported accordingly. About seven the Vice-Admiral made the signal for all captains, when he delivered to each a card containing a copy of his instructions, his situation in the line, etc. Few as these instructions were, they were amply sufficient, and no general signal was made during the action, except No. 16 – 'to engage the enemy as close as possible'; this the Vice-Admiral kept at his mast-head the whole time.

As soon as the reports had been delivered from all parts of the ship that everything was prepared for action, the men were ordered to breakfast. As the gunners' cabin, where I usually messed, was all cleared away, I went into the starboard cockpit berth, where I found one of the pilots that had been sounding the night before. He told us that they had pulled so near the enemy's ships as to hear the sentinel conversing, but returned without being discovered.

Our repast, it may fairly be supposed, under these circumstances was a slight one. When we left the berth, we had to pass all the dreadful preparations of the surgeons. One table was covered with instruments of all shapes and sizes, another, of more than usual strength, was placed in the middle of the cockpit. As I had never seen this produced before, I could not help asking the use of it, and received the answer 'that it was to cut off legs and wings upon'. One of the surgeon's men (called Loblolly Boys) was spreading yards and yards of bandages, about six inches wide.

Soon after breakfast the Vice-Admiral made signal to weigh and prepare for battle, anchoring with the sheet-cable out at the stern port.

The ships nearest the enemy were ordered to lead in and anchor abreast of the southernmost of the enemy's line, the others to follow them and pass in succession, so that our line became reversed or inverted. The *Monarch* being the last but two or three in the line, we had a good opportunity of seeing the other ships approach the enemy to commence the action. A more beautiful and solemn spectacle I never witnessed. The *Edgar* led the van, and on her approach the battery on the Isle of Amak, and three or four of the southernmost vessels, opened their fire upon her. A man-of-war under sail is at all times a beautiful object, but at such times the scene is heightened beyond the powers of description. We saw her pressing on through the enemy's fire, and manoeuvring in the midst of it to gain her station; our minds were deeply impressed with awe, and not a word was spoken throughout the ship but by the pilot and the helmsman, and their communications being chanted very much in the manner as the responses in our cathedral service, and repeated at intervals, added very much to the solemnity.

The *Edgar* was followed by the *Isis* and *Russell*, accompanied by the *Désirée* frigate. As our line extended to the northward, more of the enemy's ships opened their fire, and so on down their line, till lastly the Crown batteries got to work, and the action became general along the whole lines.[22]

Before Millard went to his place of duty at the aftermost guns, he saw the Monarch's *Captain, J. R. Mosse, on the poop, holding in his left hand Nelson's card of instructions and in his right hand a speaking trumpet. Within a few minutes of the* Monarch's *coming under fire, Captain Mosse was killed.*

Midshipman Millard was helped at the guns by Lieutenant-Colonel

Hutchinson, in charge of the troops on the ship, who:

. . . literally worked as hard as a dray horse. Every gun was at first supplied with a portion of shot, wadding, etc., close by it, and when these were expended, we applied to a reserved place by the main-mast. It immediately occurred to me that I could not be more usefully employed than conveying this supply, which would enable the stronger ones to remain at their guns, for the men wanted no stimulus to keep them to their duty, nor any direction how to perform it. The only cautions I remember to have given were hinted to me by the gunner before the action – viz., to worm the guns frequently, that no fire might remain from the old cart-ridge, to fire two round-shot in each gun, and to use nothing else while round-shot was to be had.

As I was returning from the main-mast, and was abreast of the little binnacle, a shot came in at the port under the poop ladder, and carried away the wheel, and three out of the four men stationed at it were either killed or wounded, besides one or two at the guns.[22]

An officer of the 49th Foot, Lieutenant Dennis:

. . . had just come up the companion ladder, and was going aft [when] splinters shattered his sword, which was in the sheath, into three pieces, and tore off the finger ends of his left hand. This, however, he scarcely seemed aware of, for, lifting up the sheath with his bloody fingers, he called out: 'Look here, Colonel!' On being reminded by Colonel Hutchinson of his wounded hand, he twisted his handkerchief round it, and set up a huzza, which was soon repeated throughout the ship. Dennis, though he could not act against the enemy, found means to make himself useful: he flew through every part of the ship, and when he found any of his men wounded, carried him in his arms down to the cockpit. When the carnage was greatest he encouraged his men by applauding their conduct, and he frequently began a huzza, which is of more importance than might be imagined, for the men have no other communication throughout the ship, but know when a shout is set up, it runs from deck to deck, and that their comrades are, some of them, in good spirits.[22]

The troops on board spent a frustrating time, not being called into action. There was, too, an unnecessary loss of life among them. Robert Southey was told of this, by his brother Tom, a lieutenant on the Bellona.

The commanding officer of the troops on board one of our ships asked where his men should be stationed? He was told that they could be of no use; that they were not near enough for musketry, and were not wanted at the guns; they had, therefore, better go below. This, he said, was impossible – it would be a disgrace that could never be wiped away. They were, therefore, drawn up upon the gangway, to satisfy this cruel point of honour; and there, without the possibility of annoying the enemy, they were mown down![36]

Lieutenant-Colonel Hutchinson, Midshipman Millard tells us,
... did not leave the quarter-deck, but walked backward and forward with coolness and composure, till at length, seeing the improbability of being ordered away, he begged I would employ him if I thought he could do any good. I was at that time seated on deck, cutting the wads asunder for the guns, and the Colonel, notwithstanding the danger attending his uniform breeches, sat himself down and went to work very busily. Indeed, afterwards I was often obliged to leave the charge of my guns to the Colonel, for I was now the only midshipman left upon the deck, and was therefore employed by Mr Yelland, the commanding officer, as his aide-decamp, and dispatched occasionally into all parts of the ship.[22]

Millard had seen two fellow-midshipmen badly cut by splinters, and himself suffered minor injury.

When the wheel was shot away, I was in a cloud, but being some little distance away, I did not receive any of the larger pieces. When I passed backwards and forwards between my quarters and the main-mast, I went on the opposite side to that which was engaged, and by that means probably escaped a severe wound, for as I was returning with two shot in one hand and a cheese (or packet) of wads in the other, I received a pretty smart blow on my right cheek. I dropped my shot, just as a monkey does a hot potato, and clapped my hand to the place, which I found rather bloody, and immediately ran aft to get my handkerchief out of my coat pocket. My friend Colonel Hutchinson came to me immediately and seemed really afraid lest my jaw was broken; however, after having felt it and found it all right, he let me return for my burden.[22]

On the Monarch's *main-deck, Millard found:*

. . . not a single man standing the whole way from the main-mast forward, a district containing eight guns on a side, some of which were run out ready for firing; others lay dismounted, and yet others remained as they were after recoiling.

I hastened down the fore-ladder to the lower deck, and felt really relieved to find somebody alive; from thence I reached the fore cockpit, where I was obliged to wait a few minutes for my cargo, and after this pause, I own I felt something like regret, if not fear, as I mounted the ladder on my return. This, however, entirely subsided when I saw the sun shining and the old blue ensign flying as lofty as ever. I never felt the genuine sense of glory so completely as at that moment, and if I had seen anyone attempt to haul that ensign down, I could have run aft and shot him dead in as determined a manner as the celebrated Paul Jones. I took off my hat by an involuntary motion, and gave three cheers as I jumped on the quarter-deck.[22]

Accurate casualty figures in these engagements were never forth-coming, but the most reliable estimates put the British killed and wounded as nearly 1,000 men. Only the 'Glorious First of June' and Trafalgar saw heavier British losses. The Danes had between 1,600 and 1,800 men killed and wounded.

Lives were lost when guns burst, especially on the older vessels. Briarly, master of the Bellona, *whose captain lost a leg in the action, logged succinctly:*

At 2, the fourth gun on the lower deck burst, by which there were several men killed and wounded, among the latter two lieutenants and two midshipmen; one of the main-deck beams broke, and part of the main-deck gangway blown up. At 3, the 14th gun on the lower deck burst, by which several men were killed and wounded, a great part of the main deck blown up, and 3 of the main-deck guns disabled aloft and 2 forward.[20]

Southey called the Battle of Copenhagen 'a murderous action', and Rear-Admiral Thomas Graves wrote to his brother shortly after the engagement:

I am told the Battle of the Nile was nothing to this. I am happy that my flag was not a month hoisted before I got into action, and into the hottest one that has happened the whole of the war. Considering the disadvantages of navigation, the approach of the enemy, their vast numbers of guns and mortars on both land and sea, I do not think there ever was a bolder attack. Some of our ships did not get into action, which made those who did feel it the hotter. In short, it was worthy of our gallant and enterprising Hero of the Nile. Nothing can exceed his spirit. Sir Hyde made the signal to discontinue the action before we had been at it two hours, supposing that our ships would all be destroyed. But our little Hero gloriously said, 'I will not move till we are crowned with victory, or that the Commander-in-Chief sends an officer to order me away.' And he was right, for if we had discontinued the action before the enemy struck, we should have all got aground and have been destroyed.[14]

It was Nelson rather than his Commander-in-Chief who in the main conceived and planned the attack on Copenhagen. It was Nelson who executed it, who defied an order to break off the engagement and went on to victory. And, again, it was Nelson who the day after the battle went to see the Prince Royal and to negotiate an armistice. The diplomatic battle, fought with pillow-soft words, Nelson found a more arduous undertaking than the more violent encounter in the channel. But he made a good impression on the Danes and handled his side of the negotiation well. All in all, he acted throughout the Baltic operation more like a Commander-in-Chief than did Sir Hyde Parker.

Nelson had no hatred for the Danes. It was Tsar Paul I and the Russian Fleet he had been itching to punish. It was ironical that, unkown to Nelson and Parker, the Tsar was a dead man when the attack on Copenhagen was launched – assassinated a week before. His son, Alexander, immediately adopted a less hostile policy towards Britain. The battle need not have been fought.

Nelson's prestige in England took a further leap forward. In the House of Commons, Prime Minister Addington said 'that Lord Nelson had shown himself as wise as he was brave, and proved that there may be united in the same person, the talents of the Warrior and the Statesman'. He was marked down for a viscountcy. And on 5th May the unfortunate Parker received a despatch from the Admiralty ordering him to relinquish command of the Baltic Fleet to his second in command, Lord Nelson.

The Battle of Trafalgar

21 October 1805

All agree there is but one Nelson. That he
may long continue the pride of his country,
is the fervent wish of your Lordship's truly
affectionate
St Vincent.

British Ships at the Battle of Trafalgar

(*Key numbers refer to figs. 6–8*)

WEATHER COLUMN

Victory (1)	100 guns	Vice-Admiral Lord Nelson (killed)
		Captain Thomas Masterman Hardy
Britannia (7)	100 guns	Rear-Admiral the Earl of Northesk
		Captain Charles Bullen
Téméraire (4)	98 guns	Captain Eliab Harvey
Neptune (3)	98 guns	Captain Thomas Fremantle
Conqueror (6)	74 guns	Captain Israel Pellew
Leviathan (5)	74 guns	Captain Henry Bayntun
Ajax (8)	74 guns	Lieutenant John Oilfold (acting)
Orion (10)	74 guns	Captain Edward Codrington
Minotaur (12)	74 guns	Captain Charles Mansfield
Spartiate (13)	74 guns	Captain Sir Francis Laforey, Bt.
Agamemnon (9)	64 guns	Captain Edward Berry
Africa (28)	64 guns	Captain Henry Digby

LEE COLUMN

Royal Sovereign (27)	100 guns	Vice-Admiral Cuthbert Collingwood
		Captain Edward Rotheram
Dreadnought (16)	98 guns	Captain John Conn
Prince (11)	98 guns	Captain Richard Grindall
Tonnant (24)	80 guns	Captain Charles Tyler
Mars (25)	74 guns	Captain George Duff (killed)
Belleisle (26)	74 guns	Captain William Hargood
Bellerophon (23)	74 guns	Captain John Cooke (killed)
Colossus (22)	74 guns	Captain James Morris
Achille (21)	74 guns	Captain Richard King
Swiftsure (17)	74 guns	Captain William Rutherford
Defence (14)	74 guns	Captain George Hope
Thunderer (15)	74 guns	Lieutenant John Stockham (acting)

Defiance (19)	74 guns	Captain Philip Durham
Revenge (20)	74 guns	Captain Robert Moorsom
Polyphemus (18)	64 guns	Captain Robert Redmill

FRIGATES, ETC.

Euryalus (2)	Captain the Hon. Henry Blackwood
Naiad	Captain Thomas Dundas
Phoebe	Captain the Hon. Thomas Capel
Sirius	Captain William Prowse
Pickle (schooner)	Lieutenant John Lapenotière
Entreprenante (cutter)	Lieutenant R. B. Young

French Ships at the Battle of Trafalgar

(Key numbers refer to figs. 6–8)

Bucentaure (40) (wrecked)	80 guns	Vice-Admiral Pierre de Villeneuve
		Captain J. J. Magendie
Formidable (32)	80 guns	Rear-Admiral Dumanoir le Pelley
Neptune (43)	80 guns	Commodore Esprit Maistral
Indomptable (45) (wrecked)	80 guns	Commodore J. Hubert
Scipion (30)	74 guns	Captain C. Berenger
Intrépide (31) (burnt)	74 guns	Commodore Louis Infernet
Mont Blanc (33)	74 guns	Commodore Noel La Villegris
Duguay-Trouin (34)	74 guns	Captain C. Touffet
Héros (38)	74 guns	Captain Jean Remi Poulain (killed)
Redoutable (41) (sunk)	74 guns	Captain J. J. E. Lucas
Fougueux (47) (wrecked)	74 guns	Captain L. A. Baudouin (killed)
Pluton (49)	74 guns	Commodore Cosmao Kerjulien
Algésiras (50)	74 guns	Rear-Admiral Charles Magon (killed)
Aigle (52) (wrecked)	74 guns	Captain P. P. Gourrege
Swiftsure (54) (taken)	74 guns	Captain L'H. Villemadrin
Argonaute (55) (aground)	74 guns	Captain Epron
Achille (58) (burnt)	74 guns	Captain G. de Nieport
Berwick (60) (wrecked)	74 guns	Captain J. G. F. Camas

FRIGATES, ETC.

Cornélie, Hermione, Hortense, Rhin, Thémis, Argus (brig.), *Furet* (brig.)

Spanish Ships at the Battle of Trafalgar

(Key numbers refer to figs. 6–8)

Principe de Asturias (59)	112 guns	Admiral F. C. de Gravina (mortally wounded)
		Rear-Admiral Don Antonio Escano
Santa Ana (46)	112 guns	Vice-Admiral Don I. M. de Alava (wounded)
Santissima Trinidad (39) (sunk)	112 guns	Rear-Admiral Don H. Cisneros
		Commodore Don F. de Uriarte
Rayo (35) (wrecked)	100 guns	Commodore Don E. Macdonel
Neptuno (29) (wrecked)	80 guns	Commodore Don C. Valdes
Argonauta (56) (sunk)	80 guns	Commodore Don A. Parejas
San Francisco de Asis (36) (wrecked)	74 guns	Captain Don Louis de Flores
San Agustin (37) (burnt)	74 guns	Commodore Don Felipe X. Cagigal
San Justo (42)	74 guns	Captain Don Miguel Gaston
Monarca (48) (wrecked)	74 guns	Captain Don T. Argumosa
Bahama (51) (taken)	74 guns	Captain Don D. Galiano
Montañéz (53)	74 guns	Captain Don J. Salcedo
San Ildefonso (57) (taken)	74 guns	Captain Don J. de Bargas
San Juan Nepomuceno (61) (taken)	74 guns	Captain Don Cosme Churruca
San Leandro (44)	64 guns	Captain Don J. Quevedo

Once again ill-health was to bring Nelson back to England. Relieved of his Baltic command, he landed at Yarmouth on 1 April 1801, and travelled to London in a garlanded post-chaise with six postillions dressed as Jack Tars.

He was not idle long: before the month was out he was given charge of defending the Channel waters. The danger point was Boulogne, where Bonaparte had an invasion flotilla moored. Nelson planned, but did not lead, an abortive attack on the harbour, in which 44 of his men were killed and 128 wounded.

Soon afterwards came the Treaty of Amiens, and relaxation for Nelson at Merton Place, the elegant Surrey home he had bought in 1801 to share with the Hamiltons. When war was resumed in May 1803, Nelson was appointed Commander-in-Chief of the Mediterranean Fleet, hoisting his flag on the Victory *at Portsmouth on the 16th.*

A frustrating two years followed, mostly spent off Toulon, where a French fleet refused to be drawn out to fight.

It was the familiar story of French supremacy on land and British supremacy at sea. Napoleon knew that his dream of invading England could not be realized unless the British Fleet could be drawn well away from the Channel and his own fleet established there. To this end he worked out an elaborate and unrealistic plan that expected too much of his admirals. The French warships tucked away in Toulon, under command of Rear-Admiral Pierre de Villeneuve, and others at Rochefort and Brest were to evade the British blockade and meet up with their Spanish allies, at that time in Ferrol, Cadiz, Cartagena, and at Fort Royal on the island of Martinique. Various British interests were to be attacked, after which diversion the combined French and Spanish Fleets were instructed to hasten back and protect an invasion flotilla that would cross the English Channel and land on the coast of Kent some time in August 1805.

Admiral Ganteaume failed to get his warships out of Brest, but in January 1805, the French fleet at Rochefort slipped away, and in March the fleet anchored at Toulon followed. A few weeks later the Spanish ships took off from Cadiz.

Nelson combed the Mediterranean for the enemy. Stormy weather actually forced Villeneuve back to Toulon, from where he came out again on 30th March. Finally Nelson learned that the French and Spanish Fleets were in the Atlantic, heading for the West Indies, and began the long journey of pursuit. He reached Barbados early in June, where a misdirection from General Brereton, commander of the garrison at Santa Lucia, caused Nelson to turn south instead of north as his intuition had urged him.

The enemy, too, was not without confusion. Bonaparte had modified his original complicated plan, but even so it was soon in disarray. Admiral Missiessy, with his fleet from Rochefort, had reached the rendezvous well ahead of the others. He grew tired of waiting and set off back to European waters. Villeneuve reached the West Indies and, on hearing that Nelson was following him, made the same decision as Missiessy.

Nelson again went after them. There was no chance of overtaking the enemy, but he was able to send a fast frigate ahead to London with news of Villeneuve's approach. There, orders were issued for blockading British squadrons off Rochefort and Ferrol to join, under Sir Robert Calder, and await the French 100 miles west of Cape Finisterre.

Dispirited, in poor health, and sickened by failure to make contact with the enemy, Nelson now sailed back to England in the Victory. *On arrival at Portsmouth he was told that on 22nd July, Sir Robert Calder's squadron had fought a four-hour engagement with Villeneuve's fleet. Two French warships had been captured – but otherwise the battle was indecisive. The opposing fleets were in sight of each other until the 26th, when the French made off.*

Nelson reached his home at Merton on 20 August 1805. Shortly afterwards a Danish writer, J. A. Andersen, recognized him in Pall Mall and was invited to call at Merton Place on the 26th:

I was ushered into a magnificent apartment, where Lady

Hamilton sat at a window. I at first scarcely observed his Lordship, he having placed himself immediately at the entrance. The Admiral wore a uniform emblazoned with different orders of knighthood. He received me with the utmost condescension. Chairs being provided, he sat down between Lady Hamilton and myself, and having laid my *Account of the Battle of Copenhagen* on his knee crosswise, a conversation ensued.

Lord Nelson was of middle stature, a thin body, and apparently delicate constitution. The lines of his face were hard, but the penetration of his eye threw a kind of light upon his countenance, which tempered its severity, and rendered his harsh features in some measure agreeable. His luxuriant hair flowed in graceful ringlets down his temples. His aspect commanded the utmost veneration, especially when he looked upwards. Lord Nelson had not the least pride of rank; but combined with that degree of dignity which a man of quality should have, the most engaging address in his air and manners.[1]

General the Hon. Sir Arthur Wellesley, later the Duke of Wellington, had a less favourable first impression, though one which quickly improved when he met Lord Nelson in a waiting-room at the Colonial Office, Downing Street, shortly after the Admiral's return to England:

I found, also waiting to see the Secretary of State, a gentleman, who from his likeness to his pictures and the loss of an arm, I immediately recognized as Lord Nelson. He could not know who I was, but he entered at once into conversation with me, if I can call it conversation, for it was almost all on his side and all about himself, and in, really, a style so vain and so silly as to surprise and almost disgust me.

I suppose something that I happened to say may have made him guess that I was *somebody*, and he went out of the room for a moment, I have no doubt to ask the office-keeper who I was, for when he came back he was altogether a different man, both in manner and matter. All that I had thought a charlatan style had vanished, and he talked of the state of this country and of the aspect and probabilities of affairs on the Continent with a good sense, and a knowledge of subjects both at home and abroad, that surprised me equally and more agreeably than the first part of our interview had done; in fact he talked like an officer and a statesman.

Now, if the Secretary of State had been punctual, and had admitted Lord Nelson in the first quarter of an hour, I should have had the same impression of a light and trivial character that other people have had, but luckily I saw enough to be satisfied that he was really a very superior man; but certainly a more sudden and complete metamorphosis I never saw.[9]

On 2nd September Captain Blackwood of the frigate Euryalus, *on his way to London with despatches, called at Merton Place at five in the morning. Nelson was already up and dressed. The news was that the combined French and Spanish fleet had, following the brush with Calder, refitted at Vigo, then gone on to pick up their squadron at Ferrol. Villeneuve had then tried for Brest, met with a north-eastern gale, and turned for Cadiz.*

The same day that Blackwood called at Merton Place, Napoleon, furious with Villeneuve for failing to turn up to support an invasion, broke up camp at Boulogne, and marched south-east to cope with a new threat: mobilization by Austria and Russia. At Boulogne he had reviewed an invasion army of enormous strength – 'nine miles of soldiers'. Special medals had been proofed, ready for issue on the capture of London.

Nelson followed Blackwood to London, where he was asked by Lord Barham, the First Lord, to resume his command and to pick his officers. It was made plain to Nelson that the British government wanted the Combined Fleet destroyed.

Nelson wrote to Vice-Admiral Collingwood, then off Cadiz:

I shall be with you in a very few days, and I hope you will remain Second in Command. You will change the *Dreadnought* for *Royal Sovereign*, which I hope you will like.[27]

John Theophilus Lee, who took part in the Battle of the Nile as a 10-year-old midshipman, had by now left naval service and done well in civil life in London. He was favoured by a call from Lord Nelson.

Expressing himself happy to find I was so comfortably situated, he asked me to walk with him down the Strand, as far as Salter's shop [sword-cutler and jeweller], which I was proud to do. The crowd, which waited outside Somerset House till the noble viscount came out, was very great. He was then very ill, and neither in look nor dress betokened the naval hero, having on a pair of drab green breeches, and high black gaiters, a yellow waistcoat, and a plain blue coat, with a cocked hat, quite square, a large green shade over the eye, and a gold-headed stick in his hand, yet the crowd ran before him [and] gave his Lordship repeated and hearty cheers; indeed we could hardly get to Salter's shop, so dense was the crowd. Lord Nelson said to me, 'Does not this remind you of former days at Naples, when the crowd thus pressed on me?'

On arriving at Salter's shop, the door was closed, and his Lordship inspected all his swords which had been presented at different periods, with the diamond aigrette, numerous snuff-boxes, etc.

Sir Thomas Thompson* came in at this moment, and appearing to have something to say in private to the noble lord, I received a kind and hearty handshake from the Hero of the Nile, and then withdrew.

Lord Nelson said during the conversation we had before Sir Thomas Thompson came in, 'I have still the coffin which that good fellow [Captain] Hallowell made for me on board your ship [the *Swiftsure*, after the Nile battle]; adding, 'I always keep it in my cabin.'

Little then did I think that this bright star of the naval hemisphere would so soon disappear.[18]

Lord Minto visited Merton Place on the eve of Nelson's departure, and wrote the following day:

I went yesterday to Merton. I stayed till ten at night and took a final leave of him. He is to have forty sail of the line, and a proportional number of frigates, sloops, and small vessels. This is the largest command that any admiral has had for a long time. He goes to Portsmouth tonight.

* Captain of H.M.S. *Bellona* at Copenhagen, where he lost a leg.

Lady Hamilton was in tears all yesterday; could not eat, and hardly drink, and near swooning, and all at table. It is a strange picture. She tells me nothing can be more pure and ardent than this flame.

Nelson is in many points a really great man, in others a baby.[11]

Nelson set out for Portsmouth and the Victory *late on 13th September. At one stage of the journey, while horses were being changed, he entered a prayer in his diary:*

Friday night, at half-past ten, drove from dear, dear Merton, where I left all which I hold dear in this world, to go to serve my king and country. May the great God whom I adore enable me to fulfil the expectations of my country; and if it is His good pleasure that I should return, my thanks will never cease being offered up to the throne of His mercy. If it is His good providence to cut short my days upon earth, I bow with the greatest submission, relying that He will protect those so dear to me, that I may leave behind. His will be done. Amen. Amen. Amen.[2]

On 1st October, from the Victory, *Nelson wrote to Lady Hamilton:*

It is a relief to me to take up the pen and write you a line, for I have had, about four o'clock this morning, one of my dreadful spasms, which has almost enervated me. It is very odd, I was hardly ever better than yesterday. Captain Fremantle stayed with me till eight o'clock, and I slept uncommonly well, but was awoke with this disorder. My opinion of its effect some one day has never altered. However, it is entirely gone off, and I am only quite weak, but I do assure you, my Emma, that the uncertainty of human life makes the situation of you dearer to my affectionate heart.

The good people of England will not believe that rest of body and mind is necessary for me, but perhaps this spasm may not come again these six months. I had been writing seven hours yesterday, perhaps that had some hand in bringing it upon me.

I got round Cape St Vincent the 26th, but it was the 28th before I got off Cadiz, and joined Admiral Collingwood.

I believe my arrival was most welcome, not only to the Commander of the Fleet, but almost to every individual in it; and when

I came to explain to them the '*Nelson touch*,' it was like an electric shock. Some shed tears, all approved – 'It was new – it was singular – it was simple!' and, from Admirals downwards, it was repeated – 'It must succeed, if ever they will allow us to get at them! You are, my Lord, surrounded by friends, whom you inspire with confidence.'

Some may be Judas's; but the majority are certainly much pleased with my commanding them.[33]

Nelson instructed Captain George Duff of the Mars, *on 4th October:*

As the enemy's fleets may be hourly expected to put to sea from Cadiz, I have to desire that you will keep, with the *Mars*, *Defence*, and *Colossus*, from three to four leagues between the fleet and Cadiz, in order that I may get the information from the frigates stationed off that port, as expeditiously as possible. Distant signals to be used, when flags, from the state of the weather, may not readily be distinguished in their colours. If the enemy be out, or coming out, fire guns by day or night, in order to draw my attention.

In thick weather, the ships are to close within signal of the *Victory:* one of the ships to be placed to windward, or rather to the eastward of the other two, to extend the distance of seeing; and I have desired Captain Blackwood to throw a frigate to the westward of Cadiz, for the purpose of an easy and early communication.[27]

The following day he wrote to Viscount Castlereagh:

I have only two frigates to watch them, and not one with the fleet. I am most exceedingly anxious for more *eyes*, and hope the Admiralty are hastening them to me. The last fleet was lost to me for want of frigates; God forbid this should.[27]

Vice-Admiral Collingwood was sent 'the Nelson touch' on the 9th:

My Dear Collingwood,

I send you my Plan of Attack, as far as a man dare venture to guess at the very uncertain position the enemy may be found in.

But, my dear friend, it is to place you perfectly at ease respecting my intentions, and to give full scope to your judgment for carrying them into effect. We can, my dear Collingwood, have no little jealousies. We have only one great object in view, that of annihilating our enemies, and getting a glorious peace for our country. No man has more confidence in another than I have in you: and no man will render your services more justice than your very old friend,

Nelson and Brontë.[27]

The following day Nelson sent all commanders of his ships a secret memorandum:

Thinking it almost impossible to bring a fleet of forty sail of the line into a line of battle in variable winds, thick weather, and other circumstances which must occur, without such a loss of time that the opportunity would probably be lost of bringing the enemy to battle in such a manner as to make the business decisive, I have therefore made up my mind to keep the Fleet in that position of sailing, with the exception of the First and Second in Command, that the order of sailing is to be the order of battle: placing the Fleet in two lines, of sixteen ships each with an advanced squadron of eight of the fastest-sailing two-decked ships; which will always make, if wanted, a line of twenty-four sail, on whichever line the Commander-in-Chief may direct.

The Second-in-Command will, after my intentions are made known to him, have the entire direction of his line; to make the attack upon the enemy, and to follow up the blow until they are captured or destroyed.

If the enemy's fleet should be seen to windward in line of battle, and that the two lines and advanced squadron could fetch them, they will probably be so extended that their van could not succour their rear: I should therefore probably make the Second-in-Command's signal to lead through about their twelfth ship from their rear; or wherever he could fetch, if not able to get so far advanced.

My line would lead through about their centre: and the advanced squadron to cut three or four ships ahead of their centre, so as to ensure getting at their Commander-in-Chief, on whom every effort must be made to capture.

The whole impression of the British Fleet must be to overpower from two or three ships ahead of their Commander-in-Chief (supposed to be in the centre) to the rear of their Fleet.

Something must be left to chance: nothing is sure in a sea-fight, beyond all others; shot will carry away masts and yards of friends as well as foes; but I look with confidence to a victory before the van of the enemy could succour their rear; and then that the British Fleet would most of them be ready to receive their twenty sail of the line, or to pursue them should they endeavour to make off.

If the van of the enemy tack, the captured ships must run to leeward of the British Fleet: if the enemy wear, the British must place themselves between the enemy and captured and disabled British ships: and should the enemy close, I have no fear for the result.

Captains are to look to their particular line as their rallying-point; but in case signals cannot be seen or clearly understood, no captain can do very wrong if he places his ship alongside that of an enemy.[2]

Shortly after daybreak on 19th October the British look-out ships reported a welcome sight – the enemy at Cadiz hoisting their topsails, and one after another slowly emerging from the harbour's mouth:

Sirius:
Enemy have their topsail yards hoisted.
Sirius to *Euryalus:*
Enemy are coming out of port.
Euryalus to *Phoebe:*
Enemy are coming out of port.
Phoebe to *Mars:*
Enemy are coming out of port.
Mars to *Victory:*
Enemy are coming out of port.
9.30 a.m. Victory to Fleet :
General chase, south east.[27]

Nelson's last letter:

> *Victory*, October 19th, 1805.
> Noon, Cadiz, E.S.E. 16 leagues.

My Dearest beloved Emma, the dear friend of my bosom,

The signal has been made that the enemy's combined fleet are coming out of port. We have very little wind, so that I have no hopes of seeing them before tomorrow. May the God of Battles crown my endeavours with success; at all events I will take care that my name shall ever be most dear to you and Horatia [their daughter], both of whom I love as much as my own life, and as my last writing before the battle will be to you, so I hope in God that I shall live to finish my letter after the battle. May heaven bless you prays your

> Nelson and Brontë.

October 20th. In the morning we were close to the mouth of the Straits, but the wind had not come up far enough to the westward, to allow the combined fleets to weather the shoals off Trafalgar; but they were counted as far as forty sail of ships of war, which I suppose to be thirty-four of the line and six frigates. A group of them were seen off the light-house of Cadiz this morning, but it blows so very fresh, and thick weather, that I rather believe they will go into the harbour before night. May God Almighty give us success over these fellows, and enable us to get a peace.[33]

Nelson's diary:

In the afternoon Captain Blackwood telegraphed that the enemy seemed determined to go to the westward; – and *that* they shall *not* do, if in the power of Nelson and Brontë to prevent them. At five telegraphed Captain Blackwood, that I relied upon his keeping sight of the enemy.[2]

After nightfall, a French officer reported:

Lights were continuously seen at various points of the horizon. They were the signals of the English Fleet and the look-out ships that felt the way for them. The reports of cannon, repeated from time to time, and blue lights casting a bright and sudden glare in the midst of profound darkness, were soon added to the earlier signals, and convinced Admiral Villeneuve that he would vainly attampt to conceal his course from his active foes.[13]

Captain Jean Lucas, Redoutable:

About nine o'clock at night the flagship made the general signal to the fleet to form in the order of battle at once. To carry out this evolution, those ships most to leeward ought to have shown a light at each masthead, so as to mark their positions. Whether this was done I do not know: at any rate I was unable to see such lights. At that moment, indeed, we were all widely scattered. Another cause of confusion was this. Nearly all the ships had answered the admiral's signals with flares, which made it impossible to tell which was the flagship. All I could do was to follow the motions of other ships near me, which were closing on some to leeward.

The whole fleet was by this time cleared for action, in accordance with orders signalled from the *Bucentaure* earlier in the night. In the *Redoutable*, however, we had cleared for action immediately after leaving Cadiz. A battle being certain, I kept few men on duty during the night, sending most of the officers and men to rest, so that they might be as fresh as possible for the coming fight.[13]

In contrast to French confusion, Midshipman Hercules Robinson of the Euryalus *was able to report:*

When we had brought the two fleets fairly together, we took our place between the two lines of lights, as a cab might in Regent Street, the watch was called, and Blackwood turned in quietly to wait for the morning.[13]

Nelson's diary:

Monday, October 21. At daylight saw enemy's Combined Fleets from east to E.S.E. Bore away. Made the signal for order of sailing, and to prepare for battle. The enemy with their heads to the southward.[2]

'Old Cuddy's' valet

entered the Admiral's cabin about daylight, and found him already up and dressing. He asked if I had seen the French fleet; and on my replying that I had not, he told me to look out at them, adding that, in a very short time, we should see a great deal more of them. I then observed a crowd of ships to leeward; but I could not help looking with still greater interest at the Admiral, who, during all this time, was shaving himself with a composure that quite astonished me.

Admiral Collingwood dressed himself that morning with peculiar care; and soon after, meeting Lieutenant Clavell, advised him to pull off his boots. 'You had better,' he said, 'put on silk stockings, as I have done: for if one should get a shot in the leg, they would be so much more manageable for the surgeon.'[7]

The Victory's *surgeon, Sir William Beatty, M.D., saw Nelson come* upon deck soon after daylight. He was dressed as usual in his Admiral's frock-coat, bearing on the left breast four stars of different orders which he always wore with his common apparel. (His Lordship did not wear his sword: it was laid ready on his table but it is supposed he forgot to call for it. This was the only action in which he ever appeared without a sword). He displayed excellent spirits and expressed his pleasure at the prospect of giving a fatal blow to the naval power of France and Spain; and spoke with confidence of obtaining a signal victory notwithstanding the inferiority of the British Fleet, declaring to Captain Hardy that 'he would not be contented with capturing less than twenty sail of the line.'[2]

Lord Nelson then ascended the poop, to have a better view of both lines of the British Fleet; and while there, gave particular directions for taking down from his cabin the different fixtures, and for being very careful in removing the portrait of Lady Hamilton. 'Take care of my Guardian Angel,' said he, addressing himself to the persons to be employed in the business.[2]

Shortly afterwards, Nelson went to his cabin and, kneeling, penned his last private diary entry:

At daylight, saw the enemy's combined fleets from east to E.S.E.; bore away; made the signal for Order of Sailing and to Prepare for Battle. The enemy with their heads to the southward. At seven the enemy wearing in succession.

May the Great God whom I worship, grant to my Country, and for the benefit of Europe in general, a great and glorious Victory;

and may no misconduct in anyone tarnish it; and may humanity after Victory be the predominant feature in the British Fleet. For myself, individually, I commit my life to Him who made me, and may His blessing light upon my endeavours for serving my Country faithfully. To Him I resign myself, and the just cause which is entrusted to me to defend. Amen, Amen, Amen.[33]

Nelson then added a codicil to his will, witnessed by Blackwood and Hardy:

October the twenty-first, one thousand eight hundred and five, then in sight of the combined Fleets of France and Spain, distant about ten miles.

Whereas the eminent services of Emma Hamilton, widow of the Right Honourable Sir William Hamilton, have been of the very greatest service to our King and Country, to my knowledge, without her receiving any reward from either our King or Country; – first, that she obtained the King of Spain's letter, in 1796, to his brother, the King of Naples, acquainting him of his intention to declare war against England; from which letter the Ministry sent out orders to then Sir John Jervis, to strike a stroke, if opportunity offered, against either the arsenals of Spain, or her fleets. That neither of these were done is not the fault of Lady Hamilton. The opportunity might have been offered. Secondly, the British Fleet under my command, could never have returned the second time to Egypt, had not Lady Hamilton's influence with the Queen of Naples caused letters to be wrote to the Governor of Syracuse, that he was to encourage the fleet being supplied with everything, should they put into any port in Sicily. We put into Syracuse, and received every supply, went to Egypt, and destroyed the French Fleet.

Could I have rewarded these services, I would not now call upon my Country; but as that has not been in my power, I leave Emma Lady Hamilton, therefore, a legacy to my King and Country, that they will give her an ample provision to maintain her rank in life. I also leave to the beneficence of my Country my adopted daughter, Horatia Nelson Thompson; and I desire she will use in future the name of Nelson only.

These are the only favours I ask of my King and Country at this moment when I am going to fight their Battle. May God Bless my King and Country, and all those I hold dear. My relations it is needless to mention; they will of course be amply provided for.

Nelson and Brontë.[33]

Nelson now had time to tour all parts of the Victory, *inspecting arrangements for the coming battle.*

An able-seaman's voice – John Brown of the Victory:

We cleared away our guns, whilst Lord Nelson went round the decks and said, 'My noble lads, this will be a glorious day for England, whoever lives to see it. I shan't be satisfied with twelve ships this day, as I took at the Nile.' So we piped to dinner and ate a bit of salt pork and half a pint of wine.[5]

It took nearly six hours after sighting for the British Fleet to get among the enemy. Second-Lieutenant S. B. Ellis of the Royal Marines was aboard the Ajax *in part of the attacking column Nelson led:*

There was scarcely any wind at the time, and we approached the enemy at not more than a knot and a half an hour. As we neared the French Fleet, I was sent below with orders, and was much struck with the preparations made by the blue-jackets, the majority of whom were stripped to the waist. A handkerchief was bound tightly round their heads and over the ears to deaden the noise of the cannon, many men being deaf for days after the action.

The men were variously occupied: some were sharpening their cutlasses, others polishing the guns, as though an inspection was about to take place instead of a mortal combat, whilst three or four, as if in mere bravado, were dancing a hornpipe. But all seemed deeply anxious to come to close quarters with the enemy. Occasionally they would look out of the ports and speculate as to the various ships of the enemy, many of which had been on former occasions engaged by our vessels.[12]

In the Revenge, *eighth in Collingwood's lee division, was a seaman who, using the pseudonym 'Jack Nastyface', wrote a book about the hardships of life in the navy. Here he writes of the preparations for the battle off Cape Trafalgar:*

During this time each ship was making the usual preparations, such as breaking away the Captain's and officers' cabins, and sending all the lumber below – the doctors, parson, purser and loblolly men, were also busy getting the medicine chests and bandages out, and sails prepared for the wounded to be placed on, that they might be dressed in rotation as they were taken down to the aft-cockpit.

In such a bustling, and, it may be said, trying as well as serious time, it is curious to notice the different dispositions of the British sailor. Some would be offering a guinea for a glass of grog, whilst others were making a kind of mutual verbal will, such as: 'If one of Johnny Crapeau's shots (a term given to the French) knocks my head off, you will take all my effects, and if you are killed and I am not, why, I will have yours and this is generally agreed to.'

About 11.45 a.m., Nelson ordered the hoisting of a famous signal. The moment is recounted by the Victory's *signal officer, Lieutenant John Pascoe:*

His Lordship came to me on the poop and said: 'I wish to say to the Fleet, ENGLAND CONFIDES THAT EVERY MAN WILL DO HIS DUTY' – and he added, 'You must be quick, for I have one more to make, which is for Close Action.' I replied, 'If your Lordship will permit me to substitute *expects* for *confides*, the signal will soon be completed, because the word *expects* is in the vocabulary, and *confides* must be spelt.' His Lordship replied, in haste, and with seeming satisfaction, 'That will do, Pasco, make it directly!'[27]

Nelson was greatly pleased by the signal, but it received a mixed reception among the Fleet.

It was at this time that Nelson's famous signal, ENGLAND EXPECTS EVERY MAN TO DO HIS DUTY, was hoisted at the masthead of the Admiral's ship [Lieutenant Ellis continued]. These words were requested to be delivered to the men [in the *Ajax*], and I was desired to inform them on the main deck of the Admiral's signal. Upon acquainting one of the quarter-masters of the order, he assembled the men with, 'Avast there, lads, come and hear the Admiral's words.'

When the men were mustered, I delivered, with becoming dignity, the sentence, rather anticipating that the effect on the men would be to awe them by its grandeur. Jack, however, did not appreciate it, for there were murmurs from some, whilst others in an audible whisper muttered, 'Do our duty! Of course we'll do our duty. I've always done mine, haven't you? Let us come alongside of 'em, and we will soon show whether we will do our duty!' Still, the men cheered vociferously – more, I believe, from love and admiration of their admiral and leaders, than from a full appreciation of this well-known signal.[12]

Lieutenant Pasco:

When the England Expects signal had been answered by a few ships in the Van, he ordered me to make the signal for Close Action, and to *keep it up:* accordingly, I hoisted No. 16 at the top-gallant mast-head, and there it remained until shot away.[27]

Captain Blackwood of the Euryalus *took leave of Nelson:*

'I trust, my Lord, that on my return to the *Victory*, which will be as soon as possible, I shall find your Lordship well, and in possession of twenty Prizes.' [To which Nelson replied:] 'God bless you, Blackwood, I shall never speak to you again.'[2]

The hopes of Nelson's opposite number, Rear-Admiral Pierre Charles de Villeneuve, had been that a favourable south-west gale might have taken the Allied Fleet safely to and through the Straits. Instead, light winds made an engagement unavoidable.

Villeneuve was a deeply unhappy man. He had sailed with the knowledge that he had been dismissed and that a replacement was journeying to Cadiz. At first he had written to General Decres, Minister of Marine, in all innocence:

Private letters from Bayonne inform us that Vice-Admiral Rosily is expected here, charged with a mission in Cadiz. The wisdom and experience of Vice-Admiral Rosily will be of the greatest help to me, and when he has made his study I shall have nothing to fear from his judgment of past and present events.[13]

But by the following day Villeneuve was aware of his sacking, and then he wrote:

I shall be happy to yield the first place to Rosily, if I am allowed to have the second; but it will be too hard to have to give up all hope of being vouchsafed the opportunity of proving that I am worthy of a better fate.[13]

Thus, sickened by the shame of his dismissal, and aware that Bonaparte was furious at the failures of his previous fleet movements, Villeneuve took the Combined Fleet to sea and now found himself facing a British fleet commanded by the man who had crushed a French fleet at the Nile.

Villeneuve was to acquit himself courageously and honourably in battle this day. His Order of Battle to his captains showed an intelligent anticipation of Nelson's likely mode of attack:

The British fleet will not be formed in a line of battle parallel with the Combined Fleet, according to the usage of former days. Nelson, assuming him to be, as reported, really in command, will seek to break our line, envelop our rear, and overpower with groups of his ships as many of ours as he can isolate or cut off.

All your efforts must be to assist one another, and, as far as possible, follow the movements of your admiral. You must be careful not to waste ammunition by long-range firing; wait and fight only at close quarters. At the same time you must, each captain, rely rather on your own courage and ardour for glory than on the admiral's signals. In the smoke and turmoil of battle an admiral can see very little himself; often he cannot make any signals at all.[13]

Villeneuve was right on both counts. After the battle, he explained his tactics on the morning of Trafalgar Day:

The enemy's fleet seemed to be heading *en masse* for my rear squadron; with the double object, apparently, of engaging in greatly superior force and of cutting the Combined Fleet off from Cadiz. I therefore signalled for the fleet to wear all together, and form line of battle in reverse squadron.

Through this new disposition the third squadron, under Rear-

Admiral Dumanoir, became the advance guard, with the *Neptuno* as squadron leader. I myself was in the centre of the fleet, in the *Bucentaure*, and Vice-Admiral Alava [*Santa Ana*] followed me with the second squadron. The Squadron of Observation, under the orders of Admiral Gravina [*Principe de Asturias*], formed the rear guard.[13]

The turnabout was an awkward operation, in which six ships went out of station. Captain Churruca, of the San Juan Nepomuceno, *now last in line instead of first, turned to his second-in-command: 'The fleet is doomed. The French admiral does not know his business.'*

The enemy continued to steer for us under all sail [continued Villeneuve], and at nine o'clock I was able to make out that their fleet was formed in two columns, of which one was heading directly for my flagship, and the other towards the rear of the Combined Fleet.

The wind was very light, the sea with a swell on, owing to which our formation in line was rendered very difficult to effect; but in the circumstances, considering the nature of the attack, the irregularity of our order did not seem a disadvantage, if each ship could have continued to keep to the wind and close upon the ship next ahead.

I made a signal to the leading ships to keep as close as possible to the wind and to make all sail possible. At eleven o'clock I signalled to the nearest squadron to keep closer to the wind and support the centre, the point on which the enemy now appeared to be directing his main attack. The enemy meanwhile came steadily on, though the wind was very light. They had their most powerful ships at the head of the columns.[13]

The British flagships led the two lines. Nelson had in fact agreed that the Téméraire *should precede the* Victory; *but now he refused to order a taking in of sail, and when Ḥarvey attempted to pass he was signalled astern. It was a similar story on the other column: Nelson signalled Duff to take the speedy* Mars *in front, but Collingwood, like Nelson, refused to give up his leading position.*

Collingwood's instructions had been to pass through the enemy's line at the twelfth ship from the rear; but on drawing close he saw that this was but a two-decker. Instead, he went for the huge and splendent Spanish flagship, the Santa Ana *under Admiral Alava. The French* Fougueux *moved up close to her Spanish ally, and fired the opening shot. Collingwood ordered his captain, Rotheram, to sail straight at the French ship, which gave way. Soon the* Royal Sovereign *and the* Santa Ana *were locked together by their lower yards in a death battle. The* Royal Sovereign's *opening broadside and a half against the Spanish flagship caused a fearful carnage, but immediately she had to contend with additional enemy ships: the* Fougueux, *the* Indomptable, *the* San Justo *and the* San Leandro *who were to rake the British flagship.*

The other British ships in Collingwood's column now began coming into the battle, led by the Belleisle.

A midshipman in the Royal Sovereign:

We led the Van, ran right down among them. We were alongside a great three-decker. I'm stationed at the heaviest guns in the ship, and I stuck close to one gun and poured it into her. She was so very close, it was impossible to miss her. She behaved very rascally, for when she struck first to us, she went round our bows, and when right ahead of us, up with her Ensign and raked us. But we soon brought our starboard guns to bear upon her, crash went her masts, and after that we made an eighty-four strike to us.

I looked once out of our stern ports – but I saw nothing but French and Spaniards round firing at us in all directions.

The *Belleisle* was next to us in the Action, and she kept off a good deal of fire from us – likewise the *Tonnant*.

It was shocking to see so many brave seamen mangled so, some with their heads half shot away, others with their entrails mashed, lying panting on the deck. The greatest slaughter was on the quarter-deck and poop.[39]

The 'rascally' ship who struck and then hoisted her colours again, was the Santa Ana, *flagship of Vice-Admiral Don Ignatio de Alava. The Spanish Admiral was severely wounded in the head during the battle, but the ship, though heavily damaged, later escaped into Cadiz. Collingwood was furious at the rehoisting of the colours, and held it against the Spaniards thereafter.*

The French Fougueux, *who fired the battle's opening shot, had the less enviable distinction of being in the thick of battle in both sectors: against both Collingwood's and Nelson's columns, and against both flagships at that. She first took terrible punishment from the* Royal Sovereign, Belleisle, *and others. Later, she drifted out of control to end up locked with the* Victory *and* Téméraire, *and suffered further damage and carnage.*

Captain Pierre Servaux of the Marine Artillery, master-at-arms of the Fougueux, *describes the ship's death-fight:*

The *Fougueux* had for her immediate leader the Spanish man-of-war *Santa Ana*, of 110 guns. By bad handling that ship left a gap of at least a cable across between herself and the next astern, ourselves; thus offering the enemy an easy passage through. It was just on this point that Admiral Collingwood directed his attack, as he advanced to break the line. It necessarily resulted that he crossed right in front of our bows, and so our first antagonist was Admiral Collingwood.

The *Fougueux*, 74 guns, fired the first gun in the fleet. As she did so she hoisted her colours. She continued her cannonade, firing on the English flagship, which was a greatly superior vessel in size, height, guns, and number of crew. Her main-deck and upper-deck guns could fire right down on to our decks, and in that way our upper-deck men employed in working the ship, and the infantry marksmen posted on the gangways, were without cover and entirely exposed.

We had also, according to our bad habit in the French Navy, fired over a hundred rounds from our big guns at long range before the English ship had practically snapped a gun lock. It was, indeed, not until we found ourselves side by side and yardarm to yardarm with the English flagship that she fired at all. Then she gave us a broadside from five and fifty guns and carronades, hurtling forth a storm of cannon balls, big and small, with musket-shot.

I thought the *Fougueux* was shattered to pieces – pulverized. The storm of projectiles that hurled themselves against and through the hull on the port side made the ship heel to starboard. Most of the sails and the rigging were cut to pieces, while the upper deck was swept clear of the greater number of the seamen working there, and of the soldier sharpshooters. Our gun-decks below had, however, suffered less severely. There, not more than thirty men were put *hors de combat*. This preliminary greeting, rough and brutal as it was, did not dishearten our men. A well-maintained fire showed the Englishmen that we too had guns and could use them.

The English ship having come up to us, made to break the line between us and the *Santa Ana*. The Spanish ship, in fact, during our action with the English leader, had not fired a single shot. She had stolidly kept on and continued her course without shortening sail, thus giving an easy passage through to the enemy. After that, however, by the smart handling of our captain, we managed to come within our proper distance of her; indeed, almost with our bow-sprit over his poop. By this manoeuvre we had the enemy's ship on the port quarter in such a way that whilst we could only receive a few shots from their stern guns, they were exposed to our whole broadside, raking the enemy, end-on, along all his decks. We soon saw the English vessel's mizen-mast go by the board, and then her rudder and steering gear were damaged, making the ship unmanageable. Her sails flapped loose in the wind, and her sheets and running rigging were cut to pieces by our hail of shot. For some time she ceased firing.

We now redoubled our efforts and we next saw her main-topmast come down. At that moment the English ship hoisted two signal flags at the foremast. It made us think that she was calling for help. And we were not wrong. After a little time two fresh English men-of-war came up and began to attack us; the one on the starboard quarter, the other at the stern. Under their fire, we held out for more than an hour, but they almost overpowered us with their terrible storm of round shot and a fusillade of bullets which carried death among our men.

Our mizen-mast was now shot by the board, while our spars were shot from the masts and were lying in wreckage along the sides of the ship. Then, too, fire broke out in the stern walk and the poop. We tried our best, in spite of the hail of shot, to put the fire out, and with hatches to cut adrift the mass of wrecked top-hamper from the fallen masts and yards and cordage. It lay along the ship's sides by the gun-tiers and was endangering the ship and exposing her to the most imminent risk of destruction by fire. At this moment the captain ordered me to climb outboard and see if the wreckage of the mainsail was not in danger of being set on fire from the main-deck guns. I obeyed; but as I clambered from the gangway into the chains one of the enemy fired her whole starboard broadside. The din and concussion were fearful; so tremendous that I almost fell headlong into the sea. Blood gushed from my nose and ears, but it did not prevent my carrying out my duty. Then our mainmast fell. Happily it was shot through some ten or twelve feet above the deck and fell over to port. At once we cut away the shrouds to starboard; but it was with great difficulty that in the end we were able to clear ourselves.

Our fire was well maintained all this time: though the great superiority of the heavy guns of the English ships, and their very advantageous position, decimated our men in a most fearful manner. More than half the crew had by this time been struck down, killed or wounded. Then, at length, our last remaining mast went; falling forward on to the fore part of the ship. Our flag, however, was still flying. It was the only thing left above the deck. All the same, neither our brave captain, nor a single one of our men, thought of lowering it.[13]

Following her encounter with the Royal Sovereign – *during which a midshipman saw Admiral Collingwood 'walking the break of the poop munching an apple' – the* Fougueux's *main fight had been with the* Belleisle. *After this she dropped to leeward and inflicted much damage on the* Mars. *From an eye-witness:*

The Captain of Marines on the poop, seeing that the *Fougueux* was getting into a position which would enable her to rake the *Mars*, came down to the quarter deck to mention it to Captain Duff. The want of wind rendered it impossible to alter the position of the *Mars*, nor could it with safety be attempted in regard to the enemy's other ships. Captain Duff, therefore, said to the Captain of Marines: 'Do you think our guns would bear on her?' He answered: 'I think not, but I cannot see for smoke.' 'Then,' replied the Captain, 'we must point our guns at the ships on which they can bear. I shall go and look, but the men below may see better, as there is less smoke.'

Captain Duff went to the end of the quarter-deck to look over the side, and then told his Aide-de-camp, Mr Arbuthnot, to go below, and order the guns to be pointed more aft, meaning against the *Fougueux*. He had scarcely turned round to go with these orders, when the *Fougueux* raked the *Mars*. A cannon shot killed Captain Duff, and two seamen who were immediately behind him. A ball struck the Captain on the breast, and carried off his head. His body fell on the gangway, where it was covered with a spare colour, a Union-jack, until after the action.[25]

Shortly afterwards, the Mars *received a broadside from the* Pluton, *and without masts or rigging drifted out of control. Nevertheless, she had an honour awaiting her – receiving on board the French Commander, Villeneuve, and his retinue, following surrender of the* Bucentaure.

The Fougueux, *too, drifted away, out of control, and had the misfortune to end up against both the powerful 98-gun* Téméraire, *second in Nelson's line, and the battling* Victory *and* Redoutable.

The Fougueux*'s master-at-arms continues:*

The *Téméraire* fell on board us. At once a broadside burst from her upper-deck guns and main battery, with a hot small-arms fusillade, fired right down into us. It swept our decks clear. Even then, though, our men rallied. With cries of 'a l'abordage!' repeated all over the ship, some sixty to eighty of them swarmed up on deck, armed with sabres and axes. But the huge English three-decker towered high above the *Fougueux*, and they fired down on us as they pleased with their musketry, until, at length, they boarded us. From two to three hundred of them suddenly rushed on board us, entering the ship from their chains and main-deck ports.

Our captain fell dead, shot through the heart with a musket bullet.

The few men who were left could make no resistance in the face of numbers. Resistance was out of the question, while still the enemy's murderous fire from the gangways continued. We were

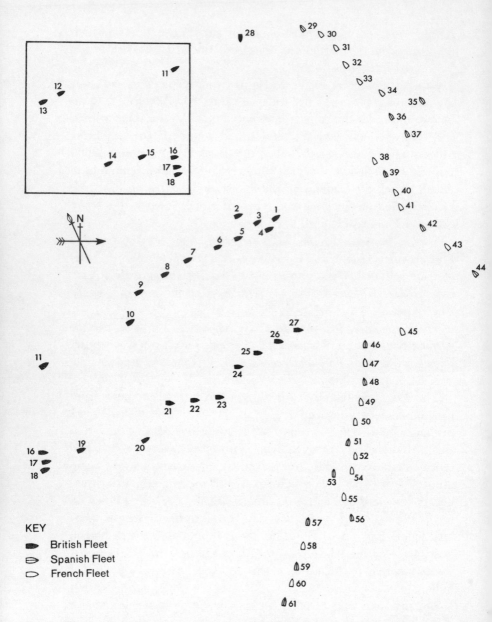

Fig. 6. The Battle of Trafalgar: position at noon. The *Royal Sovereign* opens
    fire.

obliged to give back and yield, though we defended the decks port by port. So the *Fougueux* fell into the power of the English.

Into action at the same time as the Tonnant *was the* Bellerophon, *(popularly known as the 'Billy Ruffian'). She was soon beset by several French and Spanish ships, as her log relates:*

1.35 fell on board the French two-deck ship *L'Aigle* whilst hauling to the wind, our fore-yard locking with her main yard, kept up a brisk fire both on her, on our starboard bow, and a Spanish two-decker [the *Monarca*] on the larboard bow, at the same time receiving and returning fire with a Spanish two-decker [the *Bahama*] on the larboard quarter, and receiving the fire of a Spanish two-decker [the *San Juan Nepomuceno*] athwart our stern.[20]

The L'Aigle *twice attempted to board the* Bellerophon, *whose main and mizen topmasts were brought down and her main topsail and topgallantsail set on fire. Fire caused by tossed grenades almost reached the magazine room. Her signal midshipman, John Franklin, later famous as an Arctic explorer, describes a chivalrous incident in the struggle:*

Christopher Beatty, yeoman of signals, seeing the ensign shot away a third time, mounted the mizen-rigging with the largest Union Jack he could lay his hands upon, deliberately stopped the four corners of it with as much spread as possible to the shrouds, and regained the deck unhurt. The French riflemen in the tops and on the poop of *L'Aigle*, seemingly in admiration of such daring conduct, suspended their fire for the few seconds that he remained aloft.[13]

Nevertheless, the Bellerophon *took the* Monarca, *and so damaged the* L'Aigle *that she easily fell to the freshly arriving* Defiance.

'Jack Nastyface', of the Revenge:

Our captain had given orders not to fire until we got close in with them, so that all our shot might tell; – indeed these were his words: 'we shall want all our shot when we get close in. Never mind their firing: when I fire a carronade from the quarter deck, that will be the signal for you to begin, and I know you will do your duty as Englishmen.' In a few minutes the gun was fired and our ship bore in and broke the line, but we paid dear for our temerity, as those ships we had thrown into disorder turned round and made an attempt to board. A Spanish three-decker ran her bowsprit over our poop, with a number of her crew in it, and, in her fore rigging, two or three hundred men were ready to follow; but they caught a Tartar, for their design was discovered and our marines with their small arms, and carronades on the poop, loaded with canister shot, swept them off so fast, some into the water and some on the decks, that they were glad to sheer off.

Whilst this was going on aft, we were engaged with a French two-deck ship on our starboard side, and on our larboard bow, another, so that many of their shots must have struck their own ships, and done severe execution. After being engaged about an hour, two other ships fortunately came up, received some of the fire intended for us, and we were now enabled to get at some of the shot-holes between wind and water and plug them up. This is a duty performed by the carpenter and his crew. We were now unable to work the ship, our yards, sails, and masts being disabled, and the braces completely shot away. In this condition we lay by the side of the enemy, firing away, and now and then we received a good raking from them passing under our stern. Often during the battle we could not see for the smoke whether we were firing at a foe or a friend, and as to hearing, the noise of the guns had so completely made us deaf that we were obliged to look only to the motions that were made. In this manner we continued the battle till near five o'clock when it ceased.[26]

The English Achille, *of which the* Revenge *had been astern, had taken possession of the* Berwick, *last but one in the enemy's line, after a thirty-minute engagement. The* Dreadnought *came in rather late, but forced Commodore Churruca of the* San Juan Nepomuceno, *last of the line, to strike within ten minutes. The* San Ildefonso *struck to the* Defence; *and the French* Swiftsure *and the Spanish* Bahama *struck after being heavily punished by the* Colossus *and the* Orion, *which had left Nelson's division to aid Collingwood's.*

How fared it with Nelson's weather division?

As the line had approached the Allied Fleet, which was stretched out in a crescent, Midshipman Badcock, in the Neptune, *had been impressed by the sight:*

It was a beautiful sight when their line was completed, their broadsides turned towards us, showing their iron teeth, and now and then trying the range of a shot to ascertain the distance, that they might, the moment we came within point blank (about six hundred yards), open their fire upon our van ships – no doubt with the hope of dismasting some of our leading vessels before they could close and break their lines.

Some of the enemy's ships were painted like ourselves, with double yellow sides, some with a broad single red or yellow streak, others all black, and the noble *Santissima Trinidad*, with four distinct lines of red, with a white ribbon between them, made her seem a superb man-of-war, which indeed she was. Her appearance was imposing, her head splendidly ornamented with a colossal group of figures, painted white, representing the Holy Trinity from which she took her name.[21]

Practical rather than aesthetic considerations occupied Nelson's mind. Midshipman Badcock continues:

To show the great and master mind of Nelson, who was thinking of everything even in the momentous hour of battle, it was remarked by him that the enemy had the iron hoops round their masts painted black; orders were issued by signal to whitewash those of his fleet, that in the event of all the ensigns being shot away, his ships might be distinguished by their white masts and hoops.[21]

At length the Victory *came within range of the enemy's gunfire, and seven or eight ships made her their target.*

During the forty minutes that followed [wrote Dr Beatty], the *Victory* was an unresisting target to her enemies, and her speed, slow enough at the first, decreased continually as the hail of shot riddled the sails, or stripped them from the yards. Every studding-sail boom was shot away close to the yard arms, and this light canvas, invaluable in so faint a wind, fell helplessly into the water.[2]

Twenty men were killed and 30 wounded in the Victory *before she had fired a shot.*

Dr Beatty:

Mr Scott, Public Secretary to the Commander in Chief, was killed by a cannon-shot while in conversation with Captain Hardy. Lord Nelson being then near them, Captain Adair of the Marines, with the assistance of a seaman, endeavoured to remove the body from his Lordship's sight – but he had already observed the fall of his Secretary, and now said with anxiety: 'Is that poor Scott that is gone?'

A double-headed shot struck one of the parties of Marines drawn upon the poop, and killed eight of them: his Lordship, perceiving this, ordered Captain Adair to disperse his men round the ship, that they might not suffer so much from being together.

In a few minutes afterwards a shot struck the fore-brace-bits on the quarter-deck, and passed between Lord Nelson and Captain Hardy; a splinter from the bits bruising Captain Hardy's foot, and tearing the buckle from his shoe. They both instantly stopped, and were observed by the officers on deck to survey each other with enquiring looks, each supposing the other to be wounded. His Lordship then smiled, and said: 'This is too warm work, Hardy, to last long.'[2]

The Victory's *steering wheel was shattered by enemy gunfire, and the ship steered thereafter by tackles in the gunroom. This did not deter Nelson from direct attack; and he was impatient to single out his principal target.*

Dr Beatty continues:

The enemy's van was particularly closed, having the *Santissima Trinidad* and the *Bucentaure* the ninth and tenth ships, the latter the flagship of Admiral Villeneuve; but as the admirals of the Combined Fleet declined showing their flags till the heat of battle was over, the former of these ships was only distinguished from the rest by her having four decks. Lord Nelson ordered the *Victory* to be steered for her bow.[2]

As they drew close, it was seen that three other ships were crowded together behind and beyond Villeneuve's flagship. Hardy pointed out to Nelson that he could pass close to the Bucentaure's *stern, but not round-to alongside or pass through the line without running on board*

*one of these other ships. The reply was: 'I cannot help it; it does not
signify which we run on board of. Go on board which you please: take
your choice.'*

Hardy chose to ram the Redoutable, *which proved aptly named. But
first, in passing the stern of Villeneuve's flagship, the* Victory *fired
a port forecastle carronade through her cabin windows, followed by a
double-shotted broadside that tore away the bulkheads and killed or
wounded 400 men, a blow from which the* Bucentaure *never recovered.*

To the *Victory* succeeded two others of the enemy, three-
deckers, and several seventy-fours [wrote Villeneuve]. These one
after the other came up and filed by slowly past the stern of the
Bucentaure. I had just made the signal to the van to put about
when the main and mizen masts both came down. The English
ships which had passed through astern of us were attacking us from
leeward, but, unfortunately, without suffering any serious loss in
return from our batteries. The greater part of our guns were
already dismounted and others were disabled or masked by the
fall of the masts and rigging.

Now, for one moment, the smoke-fog cleared and I saw that all
the centre and rear had given way. I found, also, that my flagship
was the most windward of all. Our foremast was still standing,
however. It offered a means for our making sail to get to leeward
to join a group of ships at a little distance which did not seem much
damaged: but immediately afterwards the foremast came down
like the others. I had had my barge kept ready, so that in the
event of the *Bucentaure* being dismasted, I might be able to go on
board some other ship, and rehoist my flag there. When the
mainmast came down I gave orders for it to be cleared for launch-
ing, but it was found to be unserviceable, damaged irreparably,
either from shot or crushed in the fall of the masts.[13]

Flag-Captain Prigny was alongside Villeneuve, and reported:

The admiral, on being told that the boat he had had prepared to
take him in case of emergency to another ship had been crushed
under the wreckage, complained bitterly that Fate had spared his
life; that amid the slaughter all round there seemed not to be one
bullet for him.[13]

Villeneuve continues:

Then I had the *Santissima Trinidad* hailed – she was just ahead of us – and asked them either to send a boat or take us in tow. But there was no answer to the hail. The *Trinidad* at that moment was hotly engaged. A three-decker was attacking her on the quarter astern, and another enemy was on the beam to leeward.

Being now without any means of repelling my antagonists, the whole of the upper deck having had to be abandoned, heaped up with dead and wounded, with the ship isolated in the midst of the enemy and unable to move, I had to yield to my destiny. It remained only to stop further bloodshed. That, already immense, could only have been in vain.[13]

From the log of the Conqueror, *one of the ships attacking the* Bucentaure:

At 2.5, the *Bucentaure* struck. Sent a boat to board her to take possession.[20]

Captain Israel Pellew of the Conqueror *could not spare his first lieutenant, but ordered Captain James Atcherley, of the Marines, to board the surrendered flagship. Not feeling he was of proper rank to receive swords from the Allied Commander-in-Chief and his two captains, Atcherley took the French officers to the nearest British ship,* Conqueror's *sister-ship, the* Mars. *But before doing so, he had secured the* Bucentaure's *magazine and observed the ghastly carnage on board:*

The dead, thrown back as they fell, lay along the middle of the deck in heaps, and the shot, passing through, had frightfully mangled the bodies. An extraordinary proportion had lost their heads. A raking shot, which entered the lower deck, had glanced along the beams and through the thickest of the people, and a French officer had declared that this shot alone had killed or disabled nearly forty men.[27]

Having delivered her crippling fire into the flagship of the enemy's Commander-in-Chief, the Victory *had then rammed the French* Redoutable, *which had closed up to the* Bucentaure *to prevent a break-through.* Victory's *studding sail boom hooked into the smaller* Redoutable's *fore-topsail. The bloody duel between these two ships was the most outstanding feature of the battle.*

Like Nelson, Captain J. J. E. Lucas of the Redoutable *was a small man physically, but in defeat at Trafalgar he had a hero's role. His was one of the few crews in the Allied Fleet trained to a discipline and efficiency comparable to that of their opponents. The smaller French ship, of 74 guns, gave the* Victory *many desperate moments, including those which took the life of England's most illustrious seaman.*

Captain Lucas survived to write an account of the Redoutable's *fight, which we join at the moment when the Combined Fleet hoisted its colours.*

The ensign of the *Redoutable* went up in a very impressive manner; the drums beat *Aux Drapeaux*; the soldiers presented arms. Then the flag was saluted by officers and men with cheers, seven times repeated, 'Vive l'Empereur!'

The enemy's column, which was directed against our centre, was on the port side, and the flagship *Bucentaure* began firing. I ordered a number of the captains of the guns to go up on the forecastle and observe why it was some of our ships fired badly. They found that all their shots carried too low and fell short. I then gave orders to aim for dismasting, and above all to aim straight.

The *Redoutable* opened fire with a shot from the first gun division. It cut through the foretopsail yard of the *Victory*, whereupon cheers and shouts resounded all over the ship. Our firing was well kept up, and in less than ten minutes the British flagship had lost her mizen-mast, foretopsail, and main topgallant mast. Meanwhile I always kept so close to the *Bucentaure* that several times they called to me from their stern gallery that I should run them down; indeed, the bowsprit of the *Redoutable* touched the crown of the flagship's taff-rail; but I assured them they had nothing to be anxious about.

The damage done to the *Victory* did not affect the daring manoeuvre of Admiral Nelson. He repeatedly persisted in trying to break the line in front of the *Redoutable*, and threatening to run us down if we opposed. But the proximity of the British flagship, though closely followed by the *Téméraire*, instead of intimidating my intrepid crew, only increased their ardour, and to show the

English Admiral that we did not fear his fouling us, I had grappling irons made fast at all the yard-arms.

The *Victory* having now succeeded in passing astern of the French admiral, ran foul of us, dropping alongside and sheering off aft in such a way that our poop lay alongside her quarter-deck. From this position the grappling irons were thrown on board her. Those at the stern parted, but those forward held on; and at the same time our broadside was discharged, resulting in a terrible slaughter. We continued to fire for some time, although there was some delay at the guns. We had to use rope rammers in several cases, and fire with the guns run in, being unable to bowse them, as the ports were masked by the sides of the *Victory*. At the same time, elsewhere, by means of muskets fired through the ports into those of the *Victory*, we prevented the enemy from loading their guns, and before long they stopped firing on us altogether. What a day of glory for the *Redoutable* if she had had to fight only with the *Victory!*

Then I became aware that the crew of the enemy were about to attempt to board us. At once I had the trumpets sounded, giving the divisional call for boarding. All hastened up from below instantly, in fine style; the officers and midshipmen sprang to the head of their men, as though at a parade. In less than a minute our decks swarmed with armed men, who spread themselves with rapidity on the poop and in the nettings and the shrouds. It would be impossible to say who was the foremost.

Then a heavy fire of musketry opened, in which Admiral Nelson fought at the head of his crew. Our firing, though, became so rapid, and was so much superior to his, that in less than a quarter of an hour we had silenced that of the *Victory* altogether. More than two hundred grenades were flung on board her, with the utmost success; her decks were strewn with the dead and wounded. Admiral Nelson was killed by the firing of our musketry.

Immediately after this, the upper deck of the *Victory* became deserted, and she again ceased firing, but it proved difficult to board her because of the motion of the two vessels, and the height of the *Victory*'s upper tier and battery. On that I gave the order to cut the supports of the main-yard so that it might serve as a bridge. At the same time Midshipman Yon and four seamen sprang on board the *Victory* by means of her anchor, and we then knew that there was nobody left in the batteries.[13]

It was at this point that two other ships also locked with Victory *and* Redoutable – *the* Fougueux, *drifting out of control from the engagement to the rear, and the British* Téméraire, *which now settled the* Redoutable's *fate with a terrible point-blank broadside.*

It is impossible to describe the carnage produced by the murderous broadside of this ship [Lucas continued in his report]. More than two hundred of our brave men were killed or wounded by it. Not being able to undertake anything on the side of the *Victory*, I now ordered the rest of the crew to man the batteries on the other side and fire at the *Téméraire* with what guns the collision when she came alongside had not dismounted. Judging by appearances, no doubt, the *Téméraire* now hailed us to surrender and not prolong a useless resistance. My reply was instantly to order some soldiers who were near me to fire back; which they did with great alacrity. At the same moment almost, the mainmast of the *Redoutable* fell on board the English ship. The topmasts of the *Téméraire* then came down, falling on board of us. Our whole poop was stove in, helm, rudder, and stern post all shattered to splinters, all the stern frame, and the decks shot through. All our guns were either smashed or dismounted by the broadsides of the *Victory* and *Téméraire*. In addition, an 18-pounder gun on the lower deck, and a 32-pounder carronade on the forecastle had burst, killing and wounding a great many men. The hull itself was riddled, shot through from side to side; deck beams were shattered; port-lids torn away or knocked to pieces. Four of our six pumps were so damaged as to be useless.

Everywhere the decks were strewn with dead men. Out of a crew of 634 men we had 522 *hors de combat*, of whom 300 were killed and 222 wounded. In the midst of this horrible carnage and devastation my splendid fellows who had not been killed, and even, too, the wounded below on the orlop deck, kept cheering, 'Long live the Emperor! We are not taken yet! Is the Captain still alive?'

I hesitated no longer about surrendering. The leaks were so serious, the enemy would not have *Redoutable* long.

I warned the *Téméraire* that if she did not at once send help and spare parts for the damaged pumps, I would have to set fire to the ship, and this would involve the *Téméraire*. The officers with some seamen and marines then took possession of the ship. One of our wounded seamen, armed with a musket and bayonet, shouted, 'I must kill another of them!' and bayoneted a British soldier in the thigh, who fell between the two vessels. In spite of this I was able to induce the party to remain on board.[13]

Despite efforts by an English party to save Redoutable – '*no toil was too hard for them*', *said Lucas – she sank the evening of the following day, in a gale-lashed sea, with a large number of wounded still on board.*

John Pollard, a 19-year-old signal midshipman, was given the name 'Nelson's Avenger'. Fifty-eight years later, a retired sea captain, he wrote to the Kentish and Surrey Mercury:

I was on the poop of the *Victory* from the time the men were beat to quarters before the action till late in the evening. I was the first struck, as a splinter hit my right arm, and I was the only officer left alive of all who had been originally stationed on the poop. It is true my old friend Midshipman Collingwood came on the poop after I had for some time discovered the men in the top of the *Redoutable;* they were in a crouching position and rose breast-high to fire. I pointed them out to Collingwood as I made my aim. He took up a musket, fired once, and then left the poop, I concluded to return to the quarter-deck, which was his station during the battle. I remained firing at the top till not a man was to be seen. The last one I discovered coming down the mizen rigging, and from my fire he fell also.[17]

About 1.35 p.m. a musket ball fired from the Redoutable's *mizen top had entered Nelson's left shoulder and penetrated to his spine. The Admiral dropped onto his knees; then, as his outstretched single arm gave way, he fell on his left side. He was carried below.*

Nelson's story from now on belongs to the Victory's *surgeon, Dr William Beatty:*

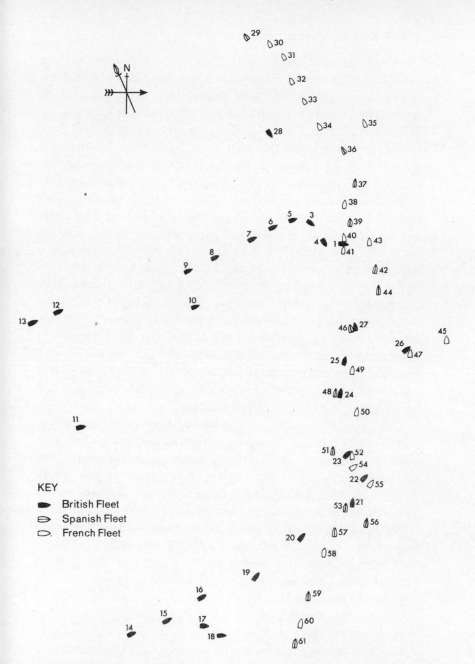

Fig. 7. The Battle of Trafalgar: position at 12.45 hours. The *Victory* cuts the line.

Several wounded officers and about forty men were likewise carried to the Surgeon for assistance just at this time and some others had breathed their last during their conveyance below. Among the latter were Lieutenant William Alexander Ram and Mr Whipple, Captain's clerk. The Surgeon had just examined these two officers, and found that they were dead, when his attention was arrested by several of the wounded calling to him, 'Mr Beatty, Lord Nelson is here; Mr Beatty, the Admiral is wounded.'

The Surgeon now, on looking round, saw the handkerchief fall from his Lordship's face; when the stars on his coat, which also had been covered by it, appeared. Mr Burke, the Purser, and the Surgeon, ran immediately to the assistance of his Lordship, and took him from the arms of the seamen who had carried him below. In conveying him to one of the midshipmen's berths, they stumbled, but recovered themselves without falling. Lord Nelson then inquired who were supporting him; and when the surgeon informed him, his Lordship replied, 'Ah, Mr Beatty, you can do nothing for me. I have but a short time to live: my back is shot through.' The Surgeon said he 'hoped the wound was not as dangerous as his Lordship imagined, and that he might still survive long to enjoy his glorious victory.'

The Reverend Doctor Scott, who had been absent in another part of the cockpit administering lemonade to the wounded, now came instantly to his Lordship; and in his anguish of grief wrung his hands, and said: 'Alas, Beatty, how prophetic you were!' alluding to the apprehensions expressed by the Surgeon for his Lordship's safety, previous to the battle.

His Lordship was laid upon a bed, stripped of his clothes, and covered with a sheet. While this was effecting, he said to Dr Scott: 'Doctor, I told you so. Doctor, I am gone!' and after a short pause, he added in a low voice: 'I have to leave Lady Hamilton and my adopted daughter Horatia, as a legacy to my Country.'

The Surgeon then examined the wound, assuring his Lordship that he would not put him to much pain in endeavouring to discover the course of the ball; which he soon found had penetrated deep into the chest, and had probably lodged in the spine. This being explained to his Lordship, he replied he was confident his back was shot through. The back was then examined externally, but without any injury being perceived; on which his Lordship was requested by the Surgeon to make him acquainted with all his sensations. He replied that 'he felt a gush of blood every minute within his breast; that he had no feeling in the lower part of his body; and that his breathing was difficult, and attended with very severe pain about that part of the spine where he was confident that the ball had struck; 'for,' said he, 'I felt it break my back.'

These symptoms, but more particularly the gush of blood which his Lordship complained of, together with the state of his pulse, indicated to the Surgeon the hopeless situation of the case; but till after the victory was ascertained and announced to his Lordship, the true nature of his wound was concealed by the Surgeon from all on board, except only Captain Hardy, Doctor Scott, Mr Burke, and Messrs Smith and Westerburgh, the Assistant Surgeons.

The *Victory*'s crew cheered whenever they observed an enemy's ship surrender. On one of these occasions, Lord Nelson anxiously inquired what was the cause of it; when Lieutenant Pasco, who lay wounded at some distance from his Lordship, raised himself up, and told him that another ship had struck: which appeared to give him much satisfaction.

He now felt an ardent thirst; and frequently called for drink, and to be fanned with paper, making use of these words: 'Fan, fan,' and 'Drink, drink.' This he continued to repeat, when he wished for drink or the refreshment of cool air, till a very few minutes before he expired. Lemonade, and wine and water were given to him occasionally.

He evinced great solicitude for the event of the battle, and fears for the safety of his friend Captain Hardy. Doctor Scott and Mr Burke used every argument they could suggest to relieve his anxiety. Mr Burke told him 'the Enemy were decisively defeated, and that he hoped his Lordship would still live to be himself the bearer of the joyful tidings to his Country'. He replied: 'It is nonsense, Mr Burke, to suppose I can live: my sufferings are

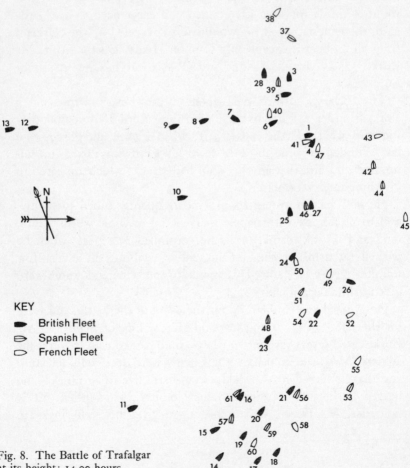

KEY

⬛ British Fleet
◨ Spanish Fleet
◫ French Fleet

Fig. 8. The Battle of Trafalgar
at its height: 14.00 hours.

great, but they will soon be over.' Doctor Scott entreated his Lordship not to despair of living, and said he trusted that Divine Providence would restore him once more to his dear Country and friends.' 'Ah, Doctor!' replied his Lordship, 'it is all over; it is all over.'

Many messages were sent to Captain Hardy by the Surgeon, requesting his attendance on his Lordship, who became impatient to see him, and often exclaimed: 'Will no one bring Hardy to me? He must be killed: he is surely destroyed.' The Captain's Aide-de-camp, Mr Bulkeley, now came below, and stated that 'circumstances respecting the Fleet required Captain Hardy's presence on deck, but that he would avail himself of the first favourable moment to visit his Lordship.' On hearing him deliver this message to the Surgeon, his Lordship inquired who had brought it. Mr Burke answered: 'It is Mr Bulkeley, my Lord.' 'It is his voice,' replied his Lordship; he then said to the young gentleman: 'Remember me to your father.'

An hour and ten minutes, however, elapsed, from the time of his Lordship's being wounded, before Captain Hardy's first subsequent interview with him; the particulars of which are nearly as follow. They shook hands affectionately, and Lord Nelson said: 'Well, Hardy, how goes the battle? How goes the day with us?' 'Very well, my Lord,' replied Captain Hardy. 'We have got twelve or fourteen of the Enemy's ships in our possession; but five of their van have tacked, and show an intention of bearing down upon the *Victory*. I have, therefore, called two or three of our fresh ships round us, and have no doubt of giving them a drubbing.' 'I hope,' said his Lordship, none of *our* ships have struck, Hardy?' 'No, my Lord,' replied Hardy, 'there is no fear of that.'

Lord Nelson then said: 'I am a dead man, Hardy. I am going fast; it will be all over with me soon. Come nearer to me. Pray let my dear Lady Hamilton have my hair, and all other things belonging to me.'

Mr Burke was about to withdraw at the commencement of this conversation; but his Lordship, perceiving his intention, desired he would remain. Captain Hardy observed, that he 'hoped

Mr Beatty could yet hold out some prospect of life.' 'Oh, no,' answered his Lordship, 'it is impossible. My back is shot through. Beatty will tell you so.' Captain Hardy then returned on deck, and at parting shook hands again with his revered friend and commander.

His Lordship now requested the Surgeon, who had been previously absent a short time attending Mr Rivers (a midshipman who lost a leg), to return to the wounded and give his assistance to such of them as he could be useful to; 'for,' said he, 'you can do nothing for me.' The Surgeon assured him that the Assistant-Surgeons were doing everything that could be effected for those unfortunate men; but on his Lordship's several times repeating his injunctions to that purpose, he left him, surrounded by Dr Scott, Mr Burke, and two of his Lordship's domestics.

After the Surgeon had been absent a few minutes attending Lieutenants Peake and Reeves of the Marines, who were wounded, he was called by Doctor Scott to his Lordship, who said: 'Ah, Mr Beatty! I have sent for you to say, what I forgot to tell you before, that all power of motion and feeling below my breast are gone; and *you*,' continued he, 'very well *know* I can live but a short time.'

The emphatic manner in which he pronounced these last words, left no doubt in the Surgeon's mind, that he adverted to the case of a man who had some months before received a mortal injury of the spine on board the *Victory*, and had laboured under similar privations of sense and muscular motion. The case had made a great impression on Lord Nelson; he was anxious to know the cause of such symptoms, which was accordingly explained to him; and he now appeared to apply the situation and fate of this man to himself. The Surgeon answered: 'My Lord, you told me so before'; but he now examined the extremities, to ascertain the fact, when his Lordship said: 'Ah, Beatty! I am too certain of it; Scott and Burke have tried it already. *You know* I am gone.' The Surgeon replied: 'My Lord, unhappily for our Country, nothing can be done for you'; and having made this declaration he was so much affected that he turned round and withdrew a few steps to conceal his emotions.

His Lordship said: 'I know it. I feel something rising in my breast,' putting his hand on his left side, 'which tells me I am gone.'

Drink was recommended liberally, and Doctor Scott and Mr Burke fanned him with paper. He often exclaimed: 'God be praised, I have done my duty'; and upon the Surgeon's inquiring whether his pain was still very great, he declared 'it continued so very severe, that he wished he was dead. Yet,' said he in a lower voice, 'one would like to live a little longer, too'; and after a pause of a few minutes, he added in the same tone: 'What would become of poor Lady Hamilton, if she knew my situation?'

The Surgeon, finding it impossible to render his Lordship any further assistance, left him, to attend Lieutenant Bligh, Messrs Smith and Westphal, Midshipmen, and some Seamen, recently wounded.

Captain Hardy now came to the cockpit to see his Lordship a second time, which was after an interval of about fifty minutes from the conclusion of his first visit. Before he quitted the deck, he sent Lieutenant Hills to acquaint Admiral Collingwood with the lamentable circumstances of Lord Nelson's being wounded. Lord Nelson and Captain Hardy shook hands again; and while the Captain retained his Lordship's hand, he congratulated him, even in the arms of death, on his brilliant victory, 'which,' said he, 'was complete; though he did not know how many of the enemy were captured, as it was impossible to perceive every ship distinctly. He was certain, however, of fourteen or fifteen having surrendered.' His Lordship answered: 'That is well, but I bargained for twenty;' and then emphatically exclaimed: '*Anchor*, Hardy, *anchor!*'

To this the Captain replied: 'I suppose, my Lord, Admiral Collingwood will now take upon himself the direction of affairs.' 'Not while I live, I hope, Hardy!' cried the dying Chief, and at that moment endeavoured ineffectually to raise himself from the bed. 'No,' added he; 'do *you* anchor, Hardy.' Captain Hardy then said: 'Shall *we* make the signal, Sir?' 'Yes,' answered his Lordship, 'for if I live, I'll anchor.'

The energetic manner in which he uttered these his last orders to Captain Hardy, accompanied with his efforts to raise himself, evinced his determination never to resign the command while he retained the exercise of his transcendent faculties, and that he expected Captain Hardy still to carry into effect the suggestion of his exalted mind; a sense of his duty overcoming the pains of death.

He then told Captain Hardy he 'felt that in a few minutes he should be no more;' adding in a low tone: 'Don't throw me overboard, Hardy.' The Captain answered: 'Oh no, certainly not.' 'Then,' replied his Lordship, 'you know what to do; and,' continued he, 'take care of my dear Lady Hamilton, Hardy. Take care of poor Lady Hamilton. Kiss me, Hardy.'

The Captain now knelt down and kissed his cheek, when his Lordship said: 'Now I am satisfied. Thank God, I have done my duty.' Captain Hardy stood for a minute or two in silent contemplation. He knelt down again, and kissed his Lordship's forehead. His Lordship said: 'Who is that?' The Captain answered: 'It is Hardy,' to which his Lordship replied: 'God bless you, Hardy!' After this affecting scene Captain Hardy withdrew, and returned to the quarter-deck, having spent about eight minutes in this his last interview with his dying friend.

Lord Nelson now desired Mr Chevalier, his Steward, to turn him upon his right side, which being effected, his Lordship said: 'I wish I had not left the deck, for I shall soon be gone.' He afterwards became very low; his breathing was oppressed, and his voice faint. He said to Doctor Scott: 'Doctor, I have not been a *great* sinner,' and after a short pause, '*Remember*, that I leave Lady Hamilton and my daughter Horatia as a legacy to my Country: and,' added he, 'never forget Horatia.'

His thirst now increased, and he called for 'drink, drink,' 'fan, fan,' and 'rub, rub,' addressing himself in the last case to Doctor Scott, who had been rubbing his Lordhip's breast with his hand, from which he found some relief. These words he spoke in a very rapid manner, which rendered his articulation difficult: but he every now and then, with evident increase of pain, made a greater effort with his vocal powers, and pronounced distinctly these last words: 'Thank God, I have done my duty;' and this great sentiment he continued to repeat so long as he was able to give it utterance.

His Lordship became speechless in about fifteen minutes after Captain Hardy left him. Doctor Scott and Mr Burke, who had all along sustained the bed under his shoulders (which raised him in nearly a semi-recumbant posture, the only one that was supportable to him), forebore to disturb him by speaking to him; and when he had remained speechless about five minutes, his Lordship's Steward went to the Surgeon, who had been a short time occupied with the wounded in another part of the cockpit, and stated his apprehensions that his Lordship was dying.

The Surgeon immediately repaired to him and found him on the verge of dissolution. He knelt down by his side and took up his hand, which was cold, and the pulse gone from the wrist. On the Surgeon's feeling his forehead, which was likewise cold, his Lordship opened his eyes, looked up, and shut them again. The Surgeon again left him and returned to the wounded who required his assistance, but was not absent five minutes before the Steward announced to him that he 'believed his Lordship had expired.'

The Surgeon returned and found that the report was too well founded; his Lordship had breathed his last, at thirty minutes past four o'clock, at which period Doctor Scott was in the act of rubbing his Lordship's breast, and Mr Burke supporting the bed under his shoulders.

From the time of his Lordship's being wounded till his death, a period of about two hours and forty-five minutes elapsed (or perhaps half an hour more): but a knowledge of the decisive victory which was gained he acquired of Captain Hardy within the first hour and a quarter of this period. A partial cannonade, however, was still maintained, in consequence of the Enemy's running ships passing the British at different points; and the last distant guns which were fired at their van ships that were making off, were heard a minute or two before his Lordship expired.[2]

The Victory's *log entered by a teenage midshipman:*

Partial firing continued until 4.30, when a victory having been reported to the Right Honourable Lord Viscount Nelson, K.B. and Commander in Chief, he then died of his wound.[20]

The immediate aftermath of a man-of-war battle was always a time of great fatigue for the seamen, and in a bloody encounter, of pitiable and horrible scenes.

'Jack Nastyface', of the Revenge:

We were now called to clear the decks, and here might be witnessed an awful and interesting scene, for as each officer and seaman would meet they were inquiring for their mess mates. Orders were now given to fetch the dead bodies from the after cockpit and throw them overboard; these were the bodies of men who were taken down to the doctor during the battle, badly wounded, and who, by the time the engagement was ended, were dead. Some of these perhaps could not have recovered while others might, had timely assistance been rendered which was impossible, for the rule is as to order requisite, that every person shall be dressed in rotation as they are brought down wounded and in many instances some have bled to death.

The next call was 'all hands to splice the main brace', which is the giving out a gill of rum to each man, and indeed they much needed it, for they had not ate or drank from breakfast time. We had now a good night's work before us; all our yards, masts, and sails were sadly cut; indeed the whole of the sails were obliged to be unbent, being rendered completely useless, and by the next morning we were partly jury-rigged.

We now began to look for our prizes, as it was coming on to blow hard on the land, and Admiral Collingwood made signals for each ship that was able to take a prize in tow, to prevent them drifting into their own harbour, as they were complete wrecks and unmanageable.[26]

Nelson's death-bed insistence on the ships anchoring was fully vindicated; a storm blew up after nightfall and lasted the most of two days. Collingwood was forced to give the order to quit the prizes after destroying or disabling them. It was the end for many splendid French and Spanish men-of-war. And with them went the British seamen's prize money.

The Revenge, *'Jack Nastyface' tells us, had taken in tow an 80-gun Spanish ship:*

Some of our men were sent on board of the Spanish ship in order to assist at the pumps, for she was much shattered in the hull between wind and water. The slaughter and havoc our guns had made rendered the scene of carnage horrid to behold; there were a number of dead bodies piled up in the hold; many, in a wounded or mutilated state, were found lying amongst them, and those who were so fortunate as to escape our shot were so dejected and crestfallen that they could not, or would not, work at the pumps, and of course the ship was in a sinking state.

The gale at this time was increasing so rapidly that manning the pumps was of no use, and we were obliged to abandon our prize, taking away with us all our men and as many prisoners as we could. On the last boat's load leaving the ship, the Spaniards who were left on board appeared on the gangway and ship's side, displaying their bags of dollars and doubloons and eagerly offering them as a reward for saving them from the expected and unavoidable wreck; but however well inclined we were, it was not in our power to rescue them, or it would have been effected without the proffered bribe.

Here, a very distressing and affecting scene took place. On quitting the ship, our boats were overloaded in endeavouring to save all the lives we could, that it is a miracle they were not upset. A father and his son came down the ship's side to get on board one of our boats; the father had already seated himself, but the men in the boat, thinking from the load and boisterous weather that all their lives would be in peril, could not think of taking the boy. As the boat put off, the lad, as though determined not to quit his father, sprang from the ship into the water, and caught hold of the gunwale of the boat; but his attempt was resisted as it risked all their lives, and some of the men resorted to their cutlasses to cut his fingers off, in order to disengage the boat from his grasp; at the same time, the feelings of the father were so worked upon, that he was about to leap overboard and perish with his son.

Britons could face an enemy, but could not witness such a scene of self-devotion . . . the crew brought father and son safe on board our ship, where they remained until, with other prisoners, they were exchanged at Gibraltar.[26]

Thirty men from the Téméraire *were still on board the* Fougueux *when the French ship perished; and other British sailors lost their lives on other prizes. It was not possible to remove all the wounded before the ships sank or were wrecked.*

Captain Lucas in the Redoutable *witnessed one part of the exhausting efforts made to save the prizes.*

During the afternoon of 22nd October:

The *Victory* separated herself from the *Redoutable*, but she was in so dismantled a state as to be *hors de combat*. It was not until seven in the evening that they were able to get the *Redoutable* clear of the *Téméraire*, which still, however, remained foul of the *Fougueux*. We had not yet been formally taken possession of, but the English *Swiftsure* now arrived and took us in tow.

We spent the whole of that night at the two pumps which were all that remained workable, without, however, being able to keep the water under. The few Frenchmen who were able to do duty joined with the English party on board in pumping, stopped several leaks, blocked up the port holes and boarded in the poop of the ship, which was ready to cave in. Indeed, no toil was too hard for them. In the middle of all the turmoil and horrible disorder on board, just keeping the ship above water, with the 'tween-decks and batteries encumbered with dead, I noticed some of my brave fellows, particularly the young midshipmen, of whom several were wounded, picking up arms which they hid on the lower decks, with the intention, as they said, of retaking the ship. Never were so many traits of intrepidity, of valour and daring, displayed on board a single ship; the whole history of our navy can show nothing like them.

Next morning the captain of the *Swiftsure* sent a boat to take me on board. At noon the *Redoutable* lost her foremast, the only mast she had left. At five in the evening the water continued so to gain on the pumps that the prize-master made signals of distress, and all the boats of the *Swiftsure* were lowered to rescue the crew. It was blowing very hard at the time, and the sea ran very high, which made the getting out of the wounded very difficult. These poor fellows, on its being seen that the ship was going down, were nearly all brought up and laid on the quarter-deck. They were able to save several of them. At seven in the evening the poop was entirely submerged. The *Redoutable* sank with a large number of the wounded still on board. They met their death with courage worthy of a better fate.[13]

In some ways the aftermath produced horrors worse than those of the battle itself.

A midshipman from the Bellerophon, *who was in the boarding party on the* Monarca, *admitted:*

I felt not the least fear of death during the action: but in the prize, when I had time to reflect upon the approach of death, I was most certainly afraid, and at one time, when the ship made three feet of water in ten minutes, when our people were almost all lying drunk upon deck, when the Spaniards, completely worn out with fatigue, would no longer work at the only chain pump left service-able, I wrapped myself up in a Union Jack and lay down upon deck.[13]

Lieutenant John Edwards of the Prince:

We had the *Santissima Trinidad*, the largest ship in the world, in tow. 'Tis impossible to describe the horrors the morning presented; nothing but signals of distress flying in every direction. The signal was made to destroy the prizes. We had no time before to remove the prisoners; but what a sight when we came to remove the wounded, of which there were between three and four hundred. We had to tie the poor mangled wretches round their waists, and lower them down into a tumbling boat, some without arms, others no legs, and lacerated all over in the most dreadful manner.[13]

Only four out of nineteen captured ships were saved; but Collingwood made sure they would be no further use to the enemy.

Shortly after the battle, he wrote to Admiral Sir Peter Parker:

You will have seen from the public accounts that we have fought a great battle, and had it not been for the fall of our noble friend, who was indeed the glory of England and the admiration of all who ever saw him in battle, your pleasure would have been perfect.

Our ships fought with a degree of gallantry that would have warmed your heart. Everybody exerted themselves, and a glorious day was made of it.

People who cannot comprehend how complicated an affair a battle at sea is, and who judge of an officer's conduct by the number of sufferers in his ship, often do him a wrong. Though there will appear great differences in the loss of men, all did admirably well; and the conclusion was grand beyond description; eighteen hulks of the enemy lying among the British Fleet without a stick standing, and the French *Achille* burning. But we were close to the rocks of Trafalgar, and when I made the signal for anchoring, many ships had their cables shot, and got an anchor ready. Providence did for us what no human effort could have done; the wind shifted a few points and we drifted off the land.

The storm being violent, and many of our ships in most perilous situations, I found it necessary to order the captures, all without masts, some without rudders, and many half full of water, to be destroyed, except such as were in better plight; for my object was their ruin and not what might be made of them.[7]

Admiral Don Federico de Gravina, though mortally wounded, had rallied what was left of the Combined Fleet and taken them into Cadiz: eleven ships – Gravina's *Principe de Asturias, the Spanish* Rayo, Montañéz, San Leandro, San Justo, *and* San Francisco de Asis; *the French* Neptune, Pluton, Argonaute, Héros, *and* Indomptable. *The* Santa Ana *had escaped also to reach Cadiz.*

Four prizes were taken into Gibraltar – the French Swiftsure, *the Spanish* Bahama, San Ildefonso, *and* San Juan Nepomuceno *– but in very poor condition. All but four of the rest of the Combined Fleet were sunk, burnt, or wrecked.*

Four enemy ships, under Rear-Admiral Dumanoir, had fled towards open sea. At 1.00 p.m. Villeneuve had put up a signal: 'Any ship that is not in action is not at her post and must take up whatever position will bring her most quickly into the firing-line.' Dumanoir, unaccountably, did not come about and engage with his advance squadron until about 3.00 p.m. by which time he had only four ships: Formidable, Scipion, Duguay-Trouin, *and* Mont Blanc. *Earlier,* Neptuno, Intrépide, *and* San Francisco de Asis *had acted independently; and the* Rayo *had become immobilized to leeward. Even so, with four fresh ships-of-the-line, Dumanoir should have troubled the crippled British ships. In fact, Dumanoir's intervention was easily repulsed, and his squadron soon fled ignominiously towards open sea. On 4th November, four British ships-of-the-line and four frigates, under Sir Richard Strachan, engaged Dumanoir's ships in the Bay of Biscay, and in a short encounter captured them. The captain of the* Duguay-Trouin *was killed, and Dumanoir himself wounded.*

Napoleon forgave neither Villeneuve nor Dumanoir. On his release from captivity and return to France in April 1806, Villeneuve locked himself in a hotel room at Rennes, stabbed himself six times with a table knife, and bled to death. Dumanoir was luckier: he was acquitted by a court martial. Bonaparte, in exile on St Helena, told a French general: 'I ought to have had Dumanoir's throat cut.'

'It was a severe action, no dodging or manoeuvring,' Collingwood said of the last, and bloodiest, of the great sailing-ship battles. The French sent a special commission to Cadiz to establish the extent of the disaster. They estimated that at Trafalgar they had 3,370 men killed and 1,160 wounded. Spanish casualties were 1,038 men killed and 1,385 wounded.

After Trafalgar, Britain's domination of the seas was not seriously challenged until 1916, at the Battle of Jutland. And Napoleon's 'naval Waterloo' prepared the way for his eventual part in that great battle on land.

Nelson's 'Apotheosis'
9 January 1806

*So early as three and four o'clock on the
morning of Thursday, thousands of people
were in motion, lest they should not reach the
places whence they intended to witness, what
may almost be termed the apotheosis of
Lord Nelson.*
THE LONDON GAZETTE

On the Victory, *immediately following the battle, Doctor William Beatty had been faced with the problem of preserving Nelson's body for what was sure to be a state funeral.*

As soon as circumstances permitted the Surgeon to devote a portion of his attention to the care of Lord Nelson's honoured remains, measures were adopted to preserve them as effectually as the means then on board the *Victory* allowed. There was no lead on board to make a coffin; a cask called a leaguer, which is of the largest size on ship-board, was chosen for the reception of the body; which, after the hair had been cut off, was stripped of the clothes except the shirt, and put into it, and the cask was then filled with brandy.

In the evening after this melancholy task was accomplished, the gale came up with violence, and continued that night and the succeeding day without any abatement. During this boisterous weather, Lord Nelson's body remained under the charge of a sentinel on the middle deck. The cask was placed on its end, having a closed aperture at its top and another below; the object of which was, that as a frequent renewal of the spirit was thought necessary, the old could thus be drawn off below and a fresh quantity introduced above, without moving the cask, or occasioning the least agitation of the body.

On the 24th there was a disengagement of air from the body to such a degree, that the sentinel became alarmed on seeing the head of the cask raised.

The spirit was drawn off at once and the cask filled again, before the arrival of the *Victory* at Gibraltar on October 28, where spirit of wine was procured; and the cask, showing a deficit produced by the body's absorbing a considerable quantity of the brandy, was then filled up with it.[2]

On 5th December the Victory *anchored at Spithead.*

Doctor Beatty continues:

As no instructions respecting his Lordship's remains were received at Portsmouth while the ship remained there, and orders being transmitted to Captain Hardy for her to proceed to the Nore, the Surgeon represented to him the necessity of examining the state of the body; common report giving reason to believe that it was intended to lie in state at Greenwich Hospital, and to be literally exposed to the public. On the day on which the *Victory* sailed from Spithead for the Nore, Lord Nelson's body was taken from the cask in which it had been kept since the day after his death. On inspecting it externally, it exhibited a state of perfect preservation, without being in the smallest degree offensive.[2]

Able seaman Brown of the Victory:

We scarce have room to move, the ship is so full of nobility coming down from London to see the ship and looking at shot holes. There is three hundred of us picked out to go to Lord Nelson's funeral. We are to wear blue jackets, white trousers, and a black scarf round our arms and hats, besides a gold medal for the Battle of Trafalgar, valued £7.1s. round our necks – that I shall take care of until I take it home.[5]

On the Victory's *leaving Spithead, Doctor Beatty began an autopsy:*

The Surgeon had, on the occasion of opening his Lordship's body, an opportunity of acquiring an accurate knowledge of the sound and healthy state of the thoracic and abdominal viscera, none of which appeared to have ever been the seat of inflammation or disease. There were no morbid indications to be seen, other than those unavoidably attending the human body six weeks after death, even under circumstances more favourable to its preservation. The heart was small, and dense in its substance, its valves, pericardium, and the large vessels, were sound and firm in their structure. The lungs were sound, and free from adhesions. The liver was very small, and its colour natural, firm in its texture, and every way free from the smallest appearance of disorganization. The stomach, as well as the spleen and other abdominal contents, were alike free from the traces of disease. Indeed all the vital parts

were so perfectly healthy in their appearance, and so small that
they resembled more those of a youth, than of a man who had
attained his forty-seventh year; which state of the body, associated
with habits of life favourable to health, gives every reason to
believe that his Lordship might have lived to a great age.[2]

However:

His Lordship had lost his right eye by a contusion which
he received at the Siege of Calvi, in the island of Corsica. The
vision of the other was likewise considerably impaired: he always
therefore wore a green shade over his forehead, to defend this eye
from the effects of strong light; but as he was in the habit of looking
much through a glass while on deck, there is little doubt, that had
he lived a few years longer, and continued at sea, he would have
lost his sight totally.[2]

*Nelson had asked to be buried in St Paul's rather than in West-
minster Abbey. He had a strange notion that the Abbey would one
day sink without trace into a swamp on which it was built.*

The London Gazette *reported:*

The noble Cathedral of St Paul had been thrown open for the
reception of visitors, at the early hour of seven in the morning.
Such, however, was the anxiety of the public to witness the
solemnities of the day, that many suffered from the pressure before
the opportunity for admission was afforded. A very short time
elapsed after the doors were opened, before the principal part of
the seats were occupied; and the interest was so deep, that no
uneasiness whatever appeared to be produced by the time which it
became necessary to wait, exposed to a great severity of cold.
From seven o'clock till one, the company sat still, and not a
symptom of impatience was discoverable.

A few minutes after one o'clock the approach of the procession
was announced, and the great western door was thrown open. At
half-past one General Sir David Dundas marched in at the head
of the Grenadier companies of the 21st and 31st Foot, and the 79th
and 92nd Highland regiments, amounting altogether to about
three hundred men. These troops moved in slow time by single
files, and formed lines on each side of the way assigned for the

procession from the western gate, along the aisle, the dome, and on to the gate of the choir. Having turned to the front, they, after some preliminary manoeuvres, were ordered to rest on their arms reversed; and in this position they remained until the whole ceremony was concluded. The appearance of this fine body of men considerably augmented the interest of the scene.

Previously to the introduction of these companies, a great part of two hundred men belonging to the West London Regiment of Militia were employed in the body of the church to guard particular seats, and to prevent any part of the crowd from getting into those places which were set apart for the accommodation of those nobility, etc., who were expected in the procession. The whole of the Militia were placed under command of the Dean, who had parties of them stationed at the several doors of the church, in order to prevent pressure or riot.

Some time had elapsed before the regiments to which the flank companies belonged had filed off to make way for the procession. The part of it which entered the church did not appear until two o'clock. It was preceded by some Marshal's men to clear the way. They were followed by two Naval Captains, the first bearing the Standard, the other the Guidon. Each was supported by two Lieutenants. Of the different degrees of rank, the Gentlemen and Esquires led the way; and among them were several of the most respectable men belonging to the commercial community. The Aldermen of London went in on the north side of the procession, and took their station opposite to the box assigned for their accommodation. His Royal Highness the Prince of Wales, accompanied by the Dukes of Clarence and Cumberland, and conducted by the Dean, walked through the church to the choir, where they remained for a short time, and then returned to join the procession. His Royal Highness the Prince of Wales took his place in the procession immediately after the Lord President of the Council (Earl Camden), and was followed by the Dukes of York, Clarence, Kent, Cumberland, Sussex, and Cambridge. The Lord Mayor and his suite were next to the Royal Dukes.

The most interesting part of the cavalcade – that which was

certainly best calculated to make a strong impression upon the minds of the spectators, was the exhibition made by the brave seamen of the *Victory*, who bore two Union Jacks, and the St George's Ensign, belonging to that ship. The colours were perforated in various places by the effects of the shot of the enemy. Several parts of the Ensign were, literally, shattered. These parts were particularly exposed to view, and the effect which such a display was calculated to produce may be more easily conceived than described.

Immediately on the van of the procession entering the great western door, the organ commenced, and an augmented choir sang an anthem.

The procession passed through the inclosed place in the centre of the dome, and of course over the grave, on its way to the choir. Although the first part entered the church about two o'clock, the whole did not reach the choir till four. It remained in the choir during the performance of evening service.

During the performance of the service in the choir, the evening approached, and lights became necessary. A number of torches were lighted up in the choir, both below and in the galleries. At the same time, the vast space under the dome was illuminated, for the first time since its construction, to a sufficient degree for the solemn purposes of the occasion. This grand central light had a most impressive and grand effect, and contributed greatly to the grandeur of a spectacle in which the burial of one of the first of Warriors and of Heroes was graced by the appearance of all the Princes of the Blood, of many of the first nobility of the land, and of an unexampled number of the subjects of His Majesty in general.

A bier, covered with black velvet, and ornamented with gold fringe and tassels, was placed in the choir, for the reception of the coffin, during the service which was performed there. About five o'clock the procession returned from the choir to the grave in an inverted order, the rear, in proceeding to the choir, forming the van on its return.

On the return of the coffin from the choir, a grand Funeral

Canopy of State was borne over it by six Admirals. It was composed of black velvet, supported by six small pillars covered with the same material, and crowned by six plumes of black ostrich feathers; the valence were fringed with black, and decorated with devices of festoons and symbols of his Lordship's victories, and his arms, crest, and coronet in gold. When the coffin was brought to the centre of the dome, it was placed on a platform sufficiently elevated to be visible from every part of the church. The state canopy was then withdrawn, and the pall taken off. The carpet and cushion on which the trophies were deposited, were laid, by the Gentleman Usher who carried them, on a table placed near the grave and behind the place which was occupied by the Chief Mourner.

Precisely at thirty-three minutes and a half past five o'clock, the coffin was lowered into the grave, by balance weight, secret machinery having been constructed expressly for the purpose.

The funeral service having been concluded in the most solemn and impressive manner, Sir Isaac Heard, Garter King at Arms, proclaimed the style and titles of the deceased Lord, in nearly the following words:

'Thus it hath pleased Almighty God to take out of this transitory life, unto his divine mercy, the Most Noble Lord Horatio Nelson, Viscount and Baron Nelson of the Nile, and of Burnham Thorpe, in the County of Norfolk, Baron Nelson of the Nile, and of Hilborough, in the same County; Knight of the Most Honourable Order of the Bath; Vice-Admiral of the White Squadron of the Fleet, and Commander-in-Chief of His Majesty's Ships and Vessels in the Mediterranean: also Duke of Brontë in Sicily; Knight Grand Cross of the Sicilian Order of St Ferdinand and of Merit; Member of the Ottoman Order of the Crescent; Knight Grand Commander of the Order of St Joachim; and the Hero who, in the moment of Victory, fell covered with immortal glory! – Let us humbly trust, that he is now raised to bliss ineffable, and to a glorious immortality.'[27]

Sources

1 Andersen, J. A., *Excursions in Britain*, 2 vols., 1809.
2 Beatty, Sir William, *Authentic Narrative of the Death of Lord Nelson*, 1807.
3 Berry, Sir Edward, *Proceedings of H.M. Squadron under the Command of Sir H. Nelson*, published anonymously 1798. Given Nicolas, Sir Nicholas Harris (Ed.), *Dispatches and Letters of Vice-Admiral Lord Viscount Nelson*, Vol. III, 1845.
4 Blanquet, Rear Admiral, 'Account of the Battle of the Nile.' Given Nicolas, Sir Nicholas Harris (Ed.), *Dispatches and Letters of Vice-Admiral Lord Viscount Nelson*, Vol. III, 1845.
5 Brown, John: Thursfield, Rear-Admiral H. G. (Ed.), *Five Naval Journals 1789–1817*, Navy Records Society, Vol. XCI.
6 Clarke, James and M'Arthur, John, *The Life and Services of Horatio Viscount Nelson*, 2 vols., 1809. An edition, published Exeter, 1902, is in 8 vols. and contains additional Nelsoniana.
7 Collingwood, Vice-Admiral Lord: Collingwood, G. L. (Ed.), *Correspondence and Memoirs of Vice-Admiral Lord Collingwood*, 1829.
8 Cordova, Don José de, 'Account of the Action with the British Squadron, on the 14th day of February, 1797,' headed 'del Oceano, the 2nd of March, at the entrance of Cadiz'. Given Ross, Sir John (Ed.), *Memoirs and Correspondence of Admiral Lord de Saumarez*, 2 vols., 1878.
9 Croker, J. W.: Jennings, L. (Ed.), *Correspondence and Diaries of J. W. Croker*, 1884.
10 Drinkwater, Colonel John (later Drinkwater-Bethune), *Narrative of St Vincent*, 1840.
11 Elliot, Sir George, quoted Fraser, E. *The Sailors Whom Nelson Led*, Methuen and Company, 1913.
12 Ellis, Lieutenant-General Sir S. B., in *Notes and Queries*, ii, 1868, p. 357.
13 Quoted in Fraser, Edward, *The Enemy at Trafalgar*, 1906.
14 Graves, Rear-Admiral Thomas, in a letter to his brother headed '*Defiance*, off the town of Copenhagen, April 3rd, 1801'. Given Jackson, Rear-Admiral Sturges (Ed.), *Logs of the Great Sea Fights*, Navy Records Society, Vol. XVIII, 1900.

15 Hood, Captain Samuel (later Vice-Admiral Sir Samuel), in a letter to Lord Hood, written on board the *Zealous* 10 August 1798. Given Jackson, Rear-Admiral Sturges (Ed.), *Logs of the Great Sea Fights*, Navy Records Society, Vol. XVIII, 1900.

16 Hoste, Captain Sir William, *Memoirs and Letters of Sir William Hoste*, 2 vols., 1833.

17 *Kentish and Surrey Mercury*, 1863.

18 Lee, John Theophilus, *Memoirs of the Life and Services of John Theophilus Lee*, 1830.

19 *Lieutenants' Certificates*, June 1762 – May 1777.

20 Log entries. Given Jackson, Rear-Admiral Sturges (Ed.), *Logs of the Great Sea Fights*, Navy Records Society, Vol. XVIII, 1900.

21 Lovell, Vice-Admiral William Stanhope (formerly Badcock), *Personal Narrative of Events from 1799 to 1815*, 1879.

22 *Macmillan's Magazine*, June 1895.

23 Miller, Captain Ralph, in a letter to his wife. Given Nicolas, Sir Nicholas Harris (Ed.), *Dispatches and Letters of Vice-Admiral Lord Viscount Nelson*, Vol. VII, cliv–clx.

24 *Naval Chronicle*, Vol. V.

25 *Naval Chronicle*, Vol. XV.

26 Nastyface, Jack (probably William Robinson), *Nautical Economy, or Forecastle Recollections*, 1836.

27 Nelson, Vice-Admiral Lord Viscount: Nicolas, Sir Nicholas Harris (Ed.), *Dispatches and Letters of Vice-Admiral Lord Viscount Nelson*, 7 vols., 1845. The leading source of Nelsoniana.

28 Nelson, Horatio, 'A Few Remarks Relative to Myself in the *Captain*, in which my pendant was flying on the most glorious Valentine's Day, 1797'. This is from the autograph draught in the Nelson Papers, as given by Nicolas. A slightly different version exists in copy in the Nelson Papers, corrected by Nelson, and with the autograph signatures of Nelson, Captain Miller, and Captain Berry.

29 Nelson, Horatio, 'Sketch of My Life'. Written for the *Naval Chronicle*, October 1799, quoted by Clarke and M'Arthur and by Nicolas.

30 Nicol, John, *Memoirs of John Nicol, Mariner*, William Blackwood, Edinburgh, 1822. A more recent edition is Laing, Alexander (Ed.), Cassell and Co., London, 1937.

31 Parker, Admiral Sir Hyde, *Journal of Admiral Sir Hyde Parker*. Given Jackson, Rear-Admiral Sturges (Ed.), *Logs of the Great Sea Fights*, Navy Records Society, Vol. XVIII, 1900.

32 Parsons, G. S., *Nelsonian Reminiscences*, 1843. First published in the *Metropolitan* magazine.

33 Pettigrew, T. J. (Ed.), *Memoirs of the Life of Vice-Admiral Lord Viscount Nelson*, 2 vols., 1849.

34 Public Records Office. Admiralty 101/123/2.
35 St Vincent, Earl: Tucker, J. S. (Ed.), *Memoirs of Earl St Vincent*, 2 vols., 1844.
36 Southey, Robert, *Life of Nelson*. Southey's classic biography is currently available in the Everyman series, J. M. Dent and Sons, London.
37 Stewart, Timothy, a pensioner at Greenwich Naval Hospital, quoted Fraser, E., *The Sailors Whom Nelson Led*. Methuen and Company, 1913.
38 Stewart, Colonel William. Nicolas, Sir Nicholas Harris (Ed.), *Dispatches and Letters of Vice-Admiral Lord Viscount Nelson*, Vol. IV, gives Stewart's narrative, taken from the Nelson Papers. Colonel Stewart was inspired to act as a self-appointed public relations officer for Nelson at Copenhagen, as another military man, Colonel Drinkwater, had done at St Vincent.
39 *The Times*, 21 October 1912.
40 Willyams, Rev. Cooper, *Voyage up the Mediterranean*, 1802.

Index